PRAYERS AND RITUALS FOR THE HOME

PRAYERS
AND RITUALS
FOR THE
Home

Celebrating the life and times of your family

KATHY HENDRICKS

DEDICATION

For my mother, Margaret,
who schooled me in the beauty of ritual,
and for my father, Albert, whose quiet faith
showed me the value of private prayer.

Twenty-Third Publications
A Division of Bayard
One Montauk Avenue, Suite 200
New London, CT 06320
(860) 437-3012 or (800) 321-0411
www.23rdpublications.com

ISBN: 978-1-58595-941-9
Library of Congress Control Number: 2013947412

Printed in the U.S.A.

Contents

All Catholic parents want to give their children the gift of a lively faith, but many of us wonder exactly how we can do that. We know that praying as a family is important, but we struggle with knowing how to make prayer time a natural part of everyday living. And this is why Kathy Hendricks's book *Prayers and Rituals for the Home* is such a valuable resource. With suggestions for daily prayers and inspiration for many different life events and stages of family life, Hendricks gives families the encouragement they need to grow together in faith. This book is practical, hands-on help for faithful families of all kinds who want to pass on the life-long gift of faith to the next generation.

DANIELLE BEAN, PUBLISHER OF *CATHOLIC DIGEST,*
THE MAGAZINE FOR FAITH AND FAMILY LIVING

Parents who want to make their family a prayerful domestic church and to teach their children to pray will be delighted with Hendricks's book. In it she provides a full buffet of ideas for prayer guaranteed to nourish the faith life of families. Suggestions include prayers that sanctify ordinary activities as well as prayers that celebrate special seasons and holidays. The clear explanations of various ways to pray and the samples provided ensure that *Prayers and Rituals for the Home* will be kept in a handy place in homes.

KATHLEEN GLAVICH, SND, AUTHOR OF *THE CATHOLIC WAY TO*
PRAY (TWENTY-THIRD PUBLICATIONS) AND *THE FISHERMAN'S*
WIFE: THE GOSPEL ACCORDING TO ST. PETER'S SPOUSE
(WESTBOW PRESS).

Opening thoughts

My family didn't pray together. Or at least not very often. Nevertheless, I learned more about prayer through my family than I have anywhere else. As a cradle Catholic, I went to Mass, if you'll pardon the pun, religiously with my parents and siblings. My Catholic schooling involved the memorization of traditional prayers and learning of devotions, such as the Rosary, but it was at home that such prayers were applied to life. My mother often reminded us of our many blessings and emphasized the importance of gratitude. When family crises hit, she sought out prayers on our behalf from a group of nuns who lived in a cloister not far from our home. Both of my parents prayed privately and, through their example, I learned the importance of bedtime prayers.

We also celebrated holidays and seasons with parties and festive meals. Our house was the central gathering place during times of transition, such as weddings and funerals. I loved the different moods that each season brought, from the bright decorations at Christmas to the easygoing routine of summer. Each one took on a particular pattern as it rolled around on the calendar once again. Without having it explained to me, I learned something about who we were as a family through the rituals we celebrated.

While prayer seems "do-able" for most families, the practice of ritual may sound a bit daunting. Stated simply, a ritual is a patterned way of doing something that involves words, symbols, or gestures. Grand rituals, such as the preparation and sharing of a Thanksgiving dinner, involve particular foods, colors, seasonal décor, and ordering of events. Who sits where at the table? How is the turkey brought in? What happens before and after the meal? Such questions point pretty clearly to the pattern involved in such a ritual and the other elements that surround it. These stem from tradition and take on greater meaning each time they are repeated. Each person knows his or her "role" and so the actions, words, gestures, and symbols don't need to be explained. We *know* through the ritual what Thanksgiving is all about.

Smaller rituals are carried out in the context of daily life. Consider the manner in which you get up in the morning and how you order the first movements of the day, such as showering, dressing, greeting others, and eating breakfast. In many instances, such activities are simply routine—they are chores that have to be done. When our actions take on a sense of purpose, however, they become more ritualistic. Savoring the first sip of coffee or the feel of a hot shower, for example, can be celebratory actions. This is why the disruption of a morning ritual feels so unsettling.

In both the grand and everyday enactment of rituals, there

is often not much thought given to how or when they started. Domestic rituals tend to evolve. This is important to consider as children move through various levels of development. Prayers and rituals that worked when they were small may become passé when they enter adolescence. The different ages and stages that make family life so full require a variety of forms and expressions of prayer. So, too, does meeting the needs, interests, and comprehension abilities of toddlers, young children, preteens, adolescents, and adults. By adapting accordingly, prayer and ritual can be both intentional and spontaneous. Having a basic knowledge and understanding of the breadth and possibility of prayer opens up possibilities for putting it into practice.

Prayer and ritual are a natural fit within families. Without even realizing it, parents communicate a great deal about spirituality through their own practice and in the way they celebrate both special and ordinary times. My intention is that this book first serve as an affirmation for what families are already doing. Then, perhaps, some of the information and suggestions that follow will provide an impetus to make these practices more deliberate.

The first chapter explores the *what* of prayer—in particular, five basic forms of prayer and ideas for bringing them into the natural flow of family life. From there it addresses *ways* to pray, including the intentional practice of meditation and contemplation as well as the spirituality folded into everyday routines. *When* to pray looks at daily prayer as well as that of seasons and holidays. The *where* of prayer takes place both in the home and outside of it, thus making the car as natural a site for prayer as the dinner table. While the benefits may seem obvious when all is going well, the *why* of prayer examines the importance of maintaining rituals and practices during mundane, difficult, or challenging times.

There are stories, suggestions, and, of course, prayers woven throughout the book. I have drawn heavily on Scripture, particularly the Psalms, for both inspiration and practical use. In addition, there are blessings, reflections, and quotes from saints and writers as well as unknown sources. I have also included a few non-Christian prayers that seemed particularly fitting. Prayers from my book, *Pocket Prayers for Parents* (Twenty-Third Publications), have been adapted to make them suitable for families to offer together. And, most especially, I have looked to Jesus for both his teaching on prayer and the example he showed through his life. What better model could we hope for?

I hope these resources and ideas serve as a jumping-off point for tailoring prayers and rituals that fit your family. Space is provided at the back of the book to write down some of your favorite family practices. However you choose to use this book, may you find the grace that unfolds with just being a family, held together in all seasons through God's love and grace.

CHAPTER 1

WHAT
to pray

M any of us learned basic prayers, such as the Our Father or a grace before meals, when we were children. These form a good foundation for a practice of prayer that lasts a lifetime. They can be said in private or with the entire family, silently or aloud. Their rhythmic pace makes them easy to draw upon when we feel tired or uninspired. Someone once described memorized prayer as old friends—they are always there when we need them.

Saying prayers, however, is only one aspect of praying. The recitation of traditional prayer is part of a much larger framework for the rich tradition of prayer in the church. So, when considering what to pray, it is helpful to start with five time-honored forms of prayer: petition, blessing, thanksgiving, praise, and intercession. Each one has tremendous potential to deepen a family's practice of prayer.

PRAYERS OF PETITION

Ask and it will be given you; search and you will find;
knock and the door will be opened for you. ⇒ MATTHEW 7:7

The ancient psalmists brought all of their concerns to God, crying out for help in times of duress and seeking comfort when confused or grief-stricken. Building on this tradition, Jesus encouraged his disciples to bring all of their needs, wants, and concerns to God, who would heed their prayers and answer them. This instruction forms the basis for prayers of *petition*. Following the example of Jesus, we bring our requests for assistance and guidance to God, trusting in his love and mercy.

By opening ourselves to the way in which God answers our prayers, we begin to recognize how richly we are blessed and can, in turn, bless others. Such recognition leads naturally to gratitude

"Acquire the habit of speaking to God as if you were alone with him. Speak with familiarity and confidence as to your dearest and most loving friend. Speak of your life, your plans, your troubles, your joys, your fears. In return, God will speak to you—not that you will hear audible words in your ears, but words that you will clearly understand in your heart."
⇒ SAINT ALPHONSUS LIGUORI

and the expression of praise for God's goodness and generosity. As our spiritual awareness expands, we turn to God not only for our own needs but also for those of others. What we pray moves outward and becomes, as a result, more open-hearted, grateful, compassionate, and aware.

Family life is full of demands upon our time, energy, and patience. The prayer of petition offers each one to God, and listens attentively for the response. Sometimes it is exactly what we were hoping for. Other times we get an answer far different from what we hoped. By incorporating petition into a family's prayer life, parents foster openness to God's love as well as a willingness to trust in God's wisdom and grace.

At times our greatest need is for healing. Thus, prayers of petition also include entreaties for forgiveness. Such prayer reminds us of our intimate connections with one another. Nowhere is this experienced more dramatically than in a family—where we acquire a knack for irritating each other, unleashing our frustrations upon one another, and sustaining grudges far past their expiration date. Asking God for forgiveness and the ability to forgive is a pathway to peace and restoration of relationships. It is prayer that changes the heart.

Rituals of Petition

Composing a Family Prayer of Petition
While there are many beautiful prayers to draw upon as a family, composing a prayer that speaks to your particular needs makes it both personal and engaging. This is especially true with prayers

of petition. Here is a simple process to get you started.

- Begin by discussing your family's immediate needs. Listen to one another and to what speaks to your hearts.
- Fill in the blanks, giving each family member a chance to add something. As you become more comfortable with the process, draw upon other prayer formulas that appeal to you, or make up one of your own.
- Offer the prayer around the dinner table, prior to attending church, or as part of a family meeting or discussion. Update the petitions on a weekly or monthly basis, or as needs shift. Purchase a journal at a local book store and use the blank pages to create more prayers.

> *Loving God,*
> *Thank you for the ways you have heard*
> *and answered our prayers,*
> *especially for* _____.
> *Help our family to be more* _____.
> *Take care of our needs, especially for* __
> _____.
> *With love and faith in you, we pray.*
> *Amen.*

Other options:
- Allow each person to name a personal petition. After each one, the family might respond, "Lord, hear our prayer."
- Place strips of paper and a pencil in a basket. Family members write out their petitions, which are then used as part

of the prayer each time it is offered.

- Before offering the prayer, take time to discuss how God has answered other petitions that the family has prayed together or individually.

Do not worry about anything, but in everything by prayer and supplication with thanksgiving let your requests be made known to God. And the peace of God, which surpasses all understanding, will guard your hearts and your minds in Christ Jesus.

— **PHILIPPIANS 4:6–7**

Family Prayer for Forgiveness

In the midst of a family conflict, it's often hard to come together and listen to one another. This prayer for forgiveness might start or cap the process of seeking reconciliation. Offer it together in order to foster understanding and reconciliation, or encourage individuals to read the prayer in solitude. Either way, be mindful of the importance of asking God to restore peace to your home and to make love the essence of your life together.

God of Mercy,
There is hurt, resentment, and anger in our home.
Show us how to settle our disagreements.
Remind us to listen to each other.
Help us to forgive each other.
Make laughter and kindness a part
of our daily lives once again.
Restore peace in our family.
Amen.

— **ADAPTED FROM** *POCKET PRAYERS FOR PARENTS*

The Jesus Prayer

One of the oldest prayers of forgiveness is the Jesus Prayer: *"Lord, Jesus Christ, have mercy on me, a sinner."* To apply the prayer to family situations, substitute the words "a sinner" for a specific petition. The prayer might then look like this:

Lord, Jesus Christ, have mercy on me...

- ...for being so impatient
- ...for not sharing with others
- ...for losing my temper
- ...for saying something hurtful

Use the prayer as a way to name the needs for forgiveness in your family as well as to foster an awareness of individual responsibility and mutual respect.

PRAYERS OF BLESSING

May you be blessed by the Lord, who made heaven and earth.
— PSALM 115:15

Blessing is another form of prayer we may have learned as children. Perhaps we offered it with others around the family table. We might have learned the Sign of the Cross, a gesture that often accompanies a blessing, as part of worship or to start and end our daily prayers. Maybe a parent or grandparent tucked us into bed and offered a prayer for a safe and secure night's sleep. Or we simply sneezed and received a handful of "bless you"s from the people within earshot.

The word "blessing" comes from the Latin word *benedicere*, which means "to say good things." In prayer, to bless is to dedicate someone or something to God, or to make something holy in God's name. To receive or bestow a blessing is an act of tenderness. It affirms the love we have been given and that we have for others and for God. When we say God has "blessed" us, we don't mean that we have simply been the recipients of good luck. Rather, we acknowledge that we are held in God's heart, cherished and beloved for who we are and not for what we do, say, or possess. No wonder that the word "blessed" is often interchanged with "happy."

> **A Blessing for a Family**
> *May God give us light to guide us, courage to support us, and love to unite us, now and evermore.*
> — SOURCE UNKNOWN

In like manner, bestowing a blessing on one another in the family is an act of love and affection. By doing so, we affirm our belief in God's benevolence, and we ask that God will care for the people we love and protect them from harm. As author Rachel Naomi Remen points out, bestowing a blessing asks God to ignite the spark of life in our lovd ones in order to bring out their intrinsic goodness and thus light the world around them.

Rituals of Blessing

Blessing a Child

A simple way to bless a child is by tracing a cross on the forehead or simply placing your hand on the child's head. Use a simple formula, such as "May God bless and protect you," and pause for a brief moment of silence.

Here are just a few of the opportunities for blessing a child or young person:

- Before bedtime
- At the start of the day
- On the first day of school
- Prior to a sporting event or recital
- When ill or after suffering an accident
- On a birthday
- Any time you want to express your love and ask for God's grace!

Bedtime blessing

Bedtime blessings provide one-on-one time with a child to discuss the day's events and ask for God's protection. Use the following ritual and prayer as is, or adapt to fit your child's age and sensibilities.

- Set aside at least 10 minutes for a bedtime ritual.
- Turn off electronic devices and eliminate other distractions. Dedicate your time and attention to your child.
- Light a vigil candle or nightlight, and let the soft glow illuminate the space around you.

Bedtime Blessing

Bless N., and watch
over him/her.
Let the day's activities
now be set aside.
Bring peace to our home.
Grant N. a restful night.
Awaken him/her in the
morning with energy
for a new day.
In gratitude for my
beloved child, I pray.
Amen.

⇒ **ADAPTED FROM *POCKET PRAYERS FOR PARENTS***

- Spend a couple of minutes listening to your child talk about his or her day. Ask what prayers he or she wants to offer before going to sleep.
- Allow time for your child to pray aloud or in silence.
- Offer a blessing for your child using a simple formula, or use a more formal prayer.
- After the blessing, assure your child of God's loving presence and extinguish the candle.

Blessings for the Home

While blessings of spiritual articles and blessings offered on behalf of the faith community are reserved for priests and bishops, it is appropriate for all of us to ask God's blessing upon the ordinary events and things that are part of our lives. This awakens us to the goodness and generosity of God and enhances our appreciation of the sacredness of the world around us.

Some ideas for blessings of the home:

- A new house or remodeled room

An Irish Blessing for a Home

Bless this house,
  O Lord, we pray.
Make it safe by night
  and day.
Bless these walls
  so firm and stout,
Keeping want
  and trouble out.
Bless the roof
  and chimney tall,
Let thy peace lie over all.
Bless the windows
  shining bright,
Letting in God's
  heavenly light.
Bless us all,
  that one day, we
May be fit to dwell
  with Thee.

⇒ SOURCE UNKNOWN

- A newly planted garden
- A newly acquired pet or one who is sick or aging
- A guestroom when preparing for company
- A kitchen prior to preparing a special meal
- A bedroom of a child or parent
- A front door as a symbol of hospitality
- A table that serves as the site of family meals and discussions
- A new phone, computer, or other electronic device
- A family car

PRAYERS OF THANKSGIVING

Rejoice always, pray without ceasing, give thanks in all circumstances... ⸺ 1 THESSALONIANS 5:16–18

It is a short step from blessing to thanksgiving. It is also a natural one. The more we become aware of God's goodness and generosity, the greater our inclination to give thanks. Little children are especially adept at this form of prayer. Ask any kindergarten teacher what happens when she invites her class to tell about the people or things for which they are grateful. The list is endless as children name everything from Grandpa to goldfish.

As we grow older, the habit of giving thanks tends to shrink rather than enlarge. Perhaps it atrophies because we become accustomed to looking at what we lack rather than embracing what we have. We live in a culture of entitlement in which we expect to be given our "due." Such an attitude kills any inclination towards gratitude; it only demands more.

A grateful heart is one of the greatest attributes a parent can encourage in a child. The benefits of gratitude are plentiful. Scientific studies have shown that grateful people have healthier immune systems and can manage stress in a more effective way. They feel more connected with others, and they boost morale among those with whom they work and play. As a spiritual discipline, the cultivation of gratitude enhances our awareness of the present moment. Brother David Steindl-Rast, who writes extensively on the spirituality of gratitude, points out that people are happy not because everything is going their way, but because they are grateful. Prayers of thanksgiving are good for body and soul.

Rituals of Thanksgiving

The FSSST Prayer

One of my favorite prayers of gratitude is something I call the FSSST prayer. I have been practicing it for years as a way to cultivate awareness of the present moment, as well as to generate gratitude for the everyday sensations that are gifts from God. The prayer consists of this:

Just before going to bed, use your fingers to identify five sensations that were part of your day:

Feeling: something you felt physically, such as a breeze that swept your cheek or holding your child's hand

Sight: something you saw that spoke of God's beautiful creation, such as a delicate flower or the lovely color of a friend's eyes

Sound: something you heard that caught your attention, such as a song wafting out of the radio or the laughter of children

Smell: some aroma that triggered a memory or association, such as popcorn at a movie theater or the fresh scent that comes with an afternoon rain

Taste: some flavor that lingered on the tongue and brought satisfaction, such as a juicy peach or pungent herb

Teaching children this prayer gives them a concrete way to recall aspects of their day that were graced by the sensate experiences of life. When practiced regularly, the prayer starts to take hold as it happens. By cultivating awareness, we start taking inventory of the feelings, sights, sounds, smells, and tastes that we experience in the moment. In such a way, we are able to practice thanksgiving at all times, just as Paul advised.

Thanksgiving in the Eucharist
Then he took a loaf of bread, and when he had given thanks, he broke it and gave it to them... ⟹ **LUKE 22:19**

In each account of Jesus breaking and sharing bread with others, both at the Last Supper and in the miracle of the loaves and fishes, he first gives thanks. The word *Eucharist* comes from a Greek word meaning "thanksgiving." Each time we, as a faith community, break and share the Bread of Life together, we give thanks and praise to God for the great gift of Jesus. We then take this with us back into our homes and communities, in order to share it with others.

Following the example of Jesus, pause before receiving or extending gifts to one another in your family. First give thanks for all that you have and are able to share. It will make gift-giving all the more joyful.

Thanksgiving in the Bible

Two mothers in the Bible serve as models of thanksgiving. After years of infertility, Hannah begged God to bless her with a child. She even made a bargain as part of this prayer: if she had a son, she promised to dedicate him to God. Hannah's prayers were answered when she gave birth to Samuel, who would grow to be a great seer and prophet. Hannah's prayer of thanksgiving (1 Samuel 2:1–10) extols God for lifting up those who are poor and despairing.

Mary responds in like fashion when she is given the news by the angel Gabriel that she will be the mother of Jesus. Her song of praise, often called the "Magnificat" (Luke 1:46–55), echoes Hannah's words of gratitude and awe in God's mercy and love. Both of these prayers provide a beautiful framework for considering the blessings God has bestowed upon us as individuals and as family. Here is an example of how lines from these and other biblical prayers of thanksgiving might be used to stimulate reflection and discussion in a family about God's grace and blessing:

"My heart exults in the Lord; my strength is exalted in my God" (1 Samuel 2:1). The word exult means to rejoice or revel in something. Name something for which you are grateful as a family. How has God strengthened you and brought you joy?

"...the Mighty One has done great things for me" (Luke 1:49). What great things has God done for you as a family? As individuals? Make a practice of naming a blessing each day that God has bestowed upon you.

"...[God] will guard the feet of his faithful ones..." (1 Samuel 2:9). How has your family been "guarded" against something threatening or devastating? In what way does God keep you safe?

We often give God thanks after a catastrophe has been diverted. Reverse the process, considering the ways God brings your family shelter and takes care of your everyday needs.

"*Surely, from now on all generations will call me blessed...*" *(Luke 1:48).* Try to look at your family from the outside in. How would others regard you as blessed? What aspects of your family life do you take for granted? Make it a practice to count your blessings on a regular basis.

Keeping a Gratitude Journal

Keeping a gratitude journal is another way to make thanksgiving a regular practice. A family might share ideas together on a daily or weekly basis and record them in the journal. The journal could also be kept in an accessible spot, such as a kitchen nook or on a coffee table, where each member of the family can make entries on his or her own. Here are some hints for making the practice work:

> *Surprise is the seed of gratefulness...Relish surprises as life's gifts.*
> ⮞ **DAVID STEINDL-RAST, OSB**

- Don't impose it on the family. Talk about the benefits of keeping the journal and get everyone's buy-in. Engage children in either creating a journal or picking one out at a local bookstore.
- Decide on a consistent time in which to record entries in the journal. Otherwise, the practice will quickly peter out.
- Be realistic about the amount of time your family has to do this. If schedules are packed, set aside a monthly gratitude get-together, perhaps over a Sunday brunch or as part of a

family outing. Read the entries together as a way to recognize the gifts God has bestowed on your family.

- Emphasize the depth of the experience over the quantity of entries. If a family member expands on one or two entries rather than jotting down random experiences, it's likely to be more meaningful.
- Encourage everyone to be attuned to surprises and the unexpected occasions for giving thanks that can arise in the course of the day.

Being Grateful during Difficult Times

In her book *The Hiding Place*, the late Corrie Ten Boom described how she, her father, and her sister Betsy harbored Jewish people in their attic during World War II to help them escape Nazi persecution and death. The Ten Booms were captured and placed in a concentration camp. Corrie and Betsy were housed in an overcrowded and dismal bunkhouse. The only ray of hope came from a nightly reading of the Bible that one of the inmates smuggled in with her belongings. When Saint Paul's exhortation to "give thanks in all circumstances" (1 Thessalonians 5:18) was read one evening, Betsy took it to heart. She urged Corrie to make this a daily practice. Corrie resisted, saying she could not give thanks for the fleas in the straw that filled their beds. Betsy insisted. Corrie prayed, albeit grudgingly, in thanksgiving for the fleas. Within a few weeks, she found out that those same fleas were the reason the guards stayed out of the bunkhouse, thus allowing the reading of the Scripture that brought such hope and consolation.

Talk about this story as a family. Use it as a way to consider the "fleas in the straw" experiences in your lives. During difficult times, keep giving thanks to God and hold on to the hope that God can and will bring something blessed out of your struggles.

PRAYER OF PRAISE

O Lord, open my lips, and my mouth will declare your praise.
— PSALM 51:15

"Fear of the Lord," one of the gifts of the Holy Spirit, might better be understood as awe. The writers of the psalms had this gift in spades. Take Psalm 148, which is often referred to as a hymn of creation. "Praise the Lord...," it begins, and then proceeds to call upon the sun, moon and stars, sea monsters and wild animals, creeping things and birds of the air, fire and hail, snow, frost, and stormy winds—all to give praise to God.

Much like thanksgiving, prayers of praise arise from recognizing the gifts of God in our midst. As one dives

> *When we are stunned to the place beyond words, we are finally starting to get somewhere.*
> — ANNE LAMOTT

deeply into spiritual waters, awe and reverence saturate the soul. Prayers of praise are our response to the glory of God. They don't involve our needs or even our gratitude. We praise God simply for being God.

Witnessing a gilded sunset or studying the intricacies of a spider's web might extract from us a simple prayer of praise that is equivalent to an alleluia: "Wow!" Author Anne Lamott notes that the prayer of wow indicates that our senses haven't dulled and that we are, instead, awakened to wonder. Parents can nurture a sense of wonder in their children by simply taking them outdoors to explore the beauty of the natural world. Whether it's a trip to a national park or to one down the block, the effect is the same. *"Let everything that breathes praise the Lord!"* (Psalm 150:6).

Rituals of Praise

Praising God in Nature

There is an actual mental psychosis called "Nature Deficit Disorder." Coined by author Richard Louv in his book *Last Child in the Woods*, it has arisen out of the continual use of television and electronic devices that keep us indoors and plugged into artificial sights and sounds. The toll this is taking on our bodies and minds is well documented. It is also inhibiting a flourishing of the soul.

Families can increase their appreciation of the natural world through the use of praise. By being open to wonder and then bringing that to prayer, praise arises naturally. Plan family outings that will take you outdoors and into places that stimulate praise: parks, zoos, forests, seashores, mountains, or gardens. Leave behind or silence cell phones and walk or sit in silence. Let yourselves breathe in the glory of God.

A Morning Psalm as Sea (INSPIRED BY THE 1928 *BOOK OF COMMON PRAYER* MORNING PRAYER)
O God, the entire universe is your holy place:
And we who see just a part of it cry out in praise:

Glory and wonder and awe!
You fill the whole of Creation.
Our hearts grow silent as we reflect upon your works,
like the calm sea in the bright morning light.

Let our words and thoughts
be honest and loving gifts to You this day, O Mover of Waves.
To You who are our strength and our hope, we pray:
*   Praise and love and delight!*
*   You set the great sun and distant stars*
dancing in the heavens
and by these steady lights, guide our way.

We are awake, O God, and our morning song is for You.
*   We are awake*
and we listen for Your voice
calling us to live this day with love and joy.

⟶ KEN PHILLIPS (ADAPTED AND USED WITH PERMISSION)

Compose a Family Psalm of Praise

Draw your family together to write your own psalm as a way to express wonder at God's goodness in your life.

- Take a blank piece of paper and write one line at the top to start the psalm, such as *"O Lord my God, you are very great"* (Psalm 104:1).
- The first person writes a line under it and folds over the top line.
- The paper is passed to the next person who reads the line above and writes another one below it.
- The top line is folded over so only the new line appears.

- The paper is thus passed around the family circle and folded, accordion-style, until all members of the family have had a chance to write something. (Parents or older siblings can help young children write a line.)

> *Keep close to Nature's heart...and break clear away, once in a while, and climb a mountain or spend a week in the woods. Wash your spirit clean.* — JOHN MUIR

- Once the psalm is finished, unfold the paper and read the psalm aloud. You may be surprised at what you hear!

Psalms of Praise

Here are some psalms of praise that you can use as part of family prayer. Offer the entire psalm together, read it in parts (one person taking a line and passing it along), or simply draw upon a single verse to pray together.

- Psalm 19—God's glory in creation and the Law
- Psalm 33—The greatness and goodness of God
- Psalm 34—Praise for deliverance from trouble
- Psalm 89—Praise for God's faithfulness
- Psalm 92—Praise for God's steadfast love
- Psalm 93—The majesty of God's rule
- Psalm 96—The glory of God
- Psalm 98—Making a joyful noise to the Lord
- Psalm 100—All lands praise God
- Psalm 103—God's goodness
- Psalm 104—The glories of creation
- Psalm 113—God, the helper of the needy

- Psalm 117—Universal call to worship God
- Psalm 135—Praise for God's goodness and might
- Psalm 139—Praise for God who knows us
- Psalm 148—Hymn of creation
- Psalm 149—Glorifying God with song
- Psalm 150—An orchestra of praise

Praising God in the Midst of Difficulty

One of the lengthiest prayers of praise in the Bible takes place, not in the beauty of the outdoors, but in the center of a furnace. Three faithful Israelites—Shadrach, Meshach, and Abednego—refuse to worship a golden idol and are sent by King Nebuchadnezzar to their deaths. Instead of being consumed by the flames, they are kept safe by God, who remains ever-faithful to them. In the Book of Daniel the three figures walk around the fiery pit singing hymns of praise to God.

Family life is not an endless stream of "oh-wow" moments. However, even in the midst of difficulty, fear, or sorrow, it is possible to continue to praise God. At such times, it can help to take a single line from the Bible and repeat it throughout a trying or tiring day. Here are some suggestions:

- *"Sing praise to God and give thanks to him, for his mercy endures forever."* (Daniel 3:90)
- *"The Lord is my strength and my might, and he has become my salvation; this is my God and I will praise him..."* (Exodus 15:2)
- *"Our God, we give thanks to you and praise your glorious name."* (1 Chronicles 29:13)
- *"O Lord, you are my God; I will exalt you, I will praise your name."* (Isaiah 25:1)

Don't tell God how big your storm is—
Tell the storm how big your God is.

≈ ANONYMOUS

PRAYERS OF INTERCESSION

I ask not only on behalf of these, but also on behalf of those who
will believe in me through their word, that they may all be one.

≈ JOHN 17:20–21

The "Final Discourse" in the Gospel of John is one of the most touching passages in the Bible. Jesus, knowing that his death is imminent, gives his disciples words of hope and comfort. Then he prays for them. It is a beautiful example of intercessory prayer.

To intercede means "to ask on behalf of." Even though we are petitioning God for help, strength, sustenance, or deliverance from harm, our prayers are turned outward and offered for others. It is a profound way to expand our spiritual horizons beyond our own needs and wants by reminding us of our interconnectedness. Therefore, what happens to one of us is felt, in some way, by all. When we pray for others, we increase our capacity for compassion. When others pray for us, we are reminded that we are not meant to go it alone. And we can always rely on the Holy Spirit to pray with and for us when we cannot do so for ourselves.

As a Christian community, we offer general intercessions as part of worship. These include prayers for leaders in the church and in the world, for those who are suffering as a result of illness, grief, or injustice, for those who have died and for those who mourn their loss. These are potent prayers, raised on behalf of those who need our collective strength.

In the Catholic tradition, prayers of intercession are also made to Mary and the saints. Prayer isn't offered "to" them—this is a common misperception about Catholic practice. Instead, we ask for their prayers on our behalf. Over the centuries, saints have been named patrons and protectors, interceding through prayer for those with special needs and guiding those with particular professions. Such prayer draws together the "communion of saints," a mystical circle of the living and the dead that reminds us that we are, as Jesus prayed, "all one."

Rituals of Intercession

Offering a Family Litany

In secular terms, a litany is a list or inventory. As a liturgical or devotional practice, it is a form of prayer that requests prayers on our behalf. As part of family prayer, a litany is a simple way to move prayer beyond requests for our own needs and concerns. By offering a series of intentions, every family member has a chance to contribute to the list of people to remember in prayer. Here are some ideas for generating your own family litany:

- Keep a sheet from a shopping notepad posted on the fridge and dedicate it to people who need prayers.
- When asked to pray for someone else, such as a friend's niece or a neighbor's parent, ask the name of the person. This makes prayers of intercession much more personal.
- Listen for people who are being prayed for at church and add them to your family litany.

- When praying the litany, add a moment of silence after each person or intention is named, or invite the entire family to respond, "Lord, hear our prayer."
- Generate bubble prayers. Name the prayer intention and then blow a bubble. As long as the bubble floats in the air, hold that person in your heart. Then repeat with the next intercession.

Praying the News

Watching or listening to the news, even for short periods at a time, can be overwhelming, alarming, and extremely depressing. Shootings, robberies, kidnapping, natural disasters, wars, famines, and examples of human cruelty prevail in the headlines. By bringing the news to our prayer, we not only give voice to our longings for peace and compassion, but we also gain a sense of perspective. This is especially

Prayer for Young Persons
God our Father,
you see your children
growing up in
an unsteady and
confusing world:
Show them that your ways
give more life than
the ways of the world,
and that following you
is better than chasing
after selfish goals.
Help them to take failure,
not as a measure
of their worth,
but as a chance
for a new start.
Give them strength to
hold their faith in you,
and to keep alive their
joy in creation;
through Jesus Christ
our Lord. Amen.
— THE BOOK OF COMMON PRAYER

important for children. By praying on behalf of our broken world, we help children place their hope and trust in God. Here is one way to "pray the news":

- Lay pages from a newspaper or news magazine on a table or the floor.
- Give each family member a colored marker and allow time to circle a headline or picture that strikes them.
- Engage in a discussion about the news events that were chosen.
- Join together in a spontaneous prayer on behalf of the people in the stories or offer a traditional prayer, such as the Our Father.
- Gather up the newspaper and, as you dispose of it, be mindful of God's power to overcome all evil with good.

*"When we are linked by the power of prayer, we,
as it were, hold each other's hand as we walk side by side
along a slippery path...The harder each one leans on the other,
the more firmly we are riveted together in love."*
— **Saint Gregory the Great**

CHAPTER 2

WAYS
to pray

O ne of the simplest and most common definitions of prayer is "talking and listening to God." This understanding recognizes that prayer is both an active and a passive process. Most of us have the talking part down pat. When it comes to listening, however, it is a different story. The *way* we pray is therefore as important as *what* we pray.

In talking to God we are most apt to use words. Whether they are memorized prayers from our religious tradition or ones that we utter spontaneously, words give expression to everyday concerns and deeper longings. The language of prayer goes beyond words, however. We also speak with our entire bodies. This makes gesture another form of prayer. By folding our hands or bowing our heads we take a stance in prayer that speaks as strongly as the words we say. Music's language offers another vibrant way to pray. Engaging, as it does, a different part of the brain, melodies and rhythms give rise to a vast array of thoughts and emotions. Whether it is joining in a cherished hymn or listening to a favorite composer, music takes prayer above and beyond words.

In order to listen, we draw upon two time-honored spiritual practices—meditation and contemplation. Each one allows the mind to settle and the heart to open. If these sound too complex for family life, consider the contemplative experience of rocking a baby to sleep and the beauty of simply being in the moment. Or of the meditative thoughts that accompany a life event, such as a high school graduation. Reflecting back on all that has brought a child to that moment opens up a broader understanding of what it means to raise a family.

In addition to what we pray, the way we pray brings new levels of awareness that give voice to our deepest needs. It also allows us to listen for God's gentle wisdom in the midst of family life.

TOOLS FOR PRAYER

I have a passion for spirituality, particularly as it applies to the home. Whenever I speak on this topic, I always emphasize the importance of silence and solitude as key practices. This isn't anything new and radical on my part; both are found in every credible spiritual tradition. Both are also becoming increasingly rare in our noisy and crowded culture. It's become commonplace when going out to eat, for example, to see multiple flat screens projecting different sporting events while loud music blares in the background. We plug ourselves into cell phones and MP3 players when walking, running, or even driving. This not only jeopardizes one's physical safety, but also does damage to the soul.

Saint Thérèse of Lisieux once noted the need to stay in touch with "holy things." These are the things that bring deeper intimacy with God. Her words resonate at a time when tablets are replacing books, and emails and texts substitute for handwritten letters. I am not opposed to any of these modern tools, but I also understand the need for those things that exist in "real time." Having grown up in a sacramental church, I know the critical importance of sensate experiences—the smell of holy oil and incense, the touch of water and the taste of eucharistic food, the sound of bells and the sight of candlelight. All of these can be manufactured in some form or other through digital means, but there is no way a virtual world will replace the actual one.

The mementoes we cherish in our families are things we make holy through associations and memory. We store them in attics and basements rather than on virtual clouds, and their meaning and worth come from the rituals and traditions with which they are connected. They symbolize stories of grace and fidelity. They are a precious connection with loved ones, reminding us that we belong to one another. Saint Thérèse knew this well. She lived a short life, but was intimately connected during those years with her family and then with her religious community. Her life reminds us that the human community is the most tangible way to see, feel, hear, taste, and be the body of Christ.

We often give little thought to objects, gestures, and words that make up family rituals. Even so, making use of blessings, actions, and objects that engage the senses brings a deeper awareness of God's presence. Some of these, such as an Advent wreath, arise out of the seasons of the church or the natural year. Others, such as blessing a child before bedtime, are wrapped into the rhythm of daily life. When considering ways to pray, deepening an appreciation for "holy things" makes prayer and ritual more intentional and meaningful.

WORDS IN PRAYER

Let the words of my mouth and the meditation of my heart be acceptable to you, O Lord, my rock and my redeemer.
⇒ PSALM 19:14

Teaching the Our Father

One of the most universal and beloved prayers is the Our Father. Given to us by Jesus, it is as much a way to pray as it is a specific prayer. Parents can and should teach this prayer to children.

In his book *Learning to Pray*, Wayne Muller points out that, in the gospels, the followers of Jesus don't ask him for *a* prayer; they ask him to teach them *how* to pray. The Our Father, or the Lord's Prayer, then follows. In like manner, parents can use this beautiful prayer as a guide to helping their children pray by listening to the lesson embedded in each line or phrase. For example:

Our Father...
One of the names we use for God is "Father." Jesus used the Aramaic word "Abba," a warmly intimate way to address God.

It is a far cry from the Greco-Roman gods who were distanced from the daily doings of humans. When helping your child pray, stress how God loves us as tenderly as a father or mother loves his or her child.

Who art in heaven...

Jesus described heaven as more a state of the heart than an actual place. God dwells in our hearts and is always accessible in prayer. Emphasize this with your child so that he or she comes to understand that God is always ready to hear our prayers.

Hallowed be thy name...

The word "hallowed" means holy, which denotes something apart from the ordinary. While God is always near to us, God is also beyond what we can know or describe. Talk to your child about being respectful when using God's name, and nurture a sense of reverence for the sanctity of God's creation.

> The [Our Father] is a guide, a teaching story, a finely crafted sequence of instructions on how to pray.
> — WAYNE MULLER

Thy Kingdom come, thy will be done on earth as it is in heaven...

Sometimes our prayers are answered in ways much different than we expected. Jesus taught us to place our trust in God, whose will for us is always for the good. Point out how this has been true in your family, and how to keep prayer open to God's broader vision.

Give us this day our daily bread...

Our "daily bread" is more than just food. We ask God to take care of us in body, mind, heart, and soul. Stress the importance of offering thanks for all that God gives us, even if it doesn't always match what we think we need.

**Forgive us our trespasses as we forgive those
who trespass against us...**

To trespass is to invade someone else's space. This is something we do when we trample on each other's feelings. Teach your child to ask for forgiveness in prayer as well as for the strength and will to forgive others.

Lead us not into temptation...

Jesus was tempted in the desert to choose things that might have brought momentary comfort or power over others. He resisted those temptations and chose, instead, to follow the way of love. Encourage your child to listen for how God wants him/her to live well and to make choices that will follow that path.

But deliver us from evil.

There are many things to fear in this world. To prevent fear from overtaking us, Jesus invites us to trust in God's protective presence. Reassure your child about God's love and care, and urge him/her to bring their fears to God in prayer.

Prayers of the Saints

The holy men and women who came before us offer ways to pray through poetic words and images. Here are some prayers your family can use for specific times and occasions:

Prayer of Saint Patrick

Incorporate gestures into this prayer as a way to make it more active. Use the prayer to celebrate Saint Patrick's Day or any time you want to increase your awareness of Christ's presence.

Christ be with me [arms crossed over chest]
Christ be within me [hands on each side of the face]
Christ behind me [hands extended, palms up, behind back]
Christ before me [hands extended, palms up, in front]
Christ beside me [one hand extended at a time to each side]
Christ to win me [hands clasped overhead]
Christ to comfort and restore me [hug self]
Christ beneath me [bend over, sweep hands outward toward
  the ground]
Christ above me [straighten up, hands extended overhead]
Christ in hearts [hands crossed over heart]
Of all that love me [arms open, swivel around to gesture to-
  wards those around you]

Prayer of Saint Teresa of Avila

This is a good nighttime prayer to pray together or in quiet when worried, anxious, or fearful.

Let nothing disturb you

nothing affright you;
everything will pass,
God never changes.
Patience attains all;
whoever has God lacks nothing;
only God suffices.

Prayer of Saint Francis

This familiar prayer is perfect for bringing a family together in times of difficulty or conflict. Because of its structure, the prayer can be offered, one line at a time, by different family members.

Lord, make me an instrument of your peace;
where there is hatred, let me sow love;
where there is injury, pardon;
where there is doubt, faith;
where there is despair, hope;
where there is darkness, light;
where there is sadness, joy.
O divine Master, grant that I may not so much seek
    to be consoled
as to console,
to be understood as to understand,
to be loved as to love.
For it is giving that we receive,
it is in pardoning that we are pardoned,
it is in dying that we are born to eternal life.
Amen.

Prayer of Saint Augustine

Images of the sea abound in the prayers of the saints. This prayer is well-suited to the seeking of peace and safety as a family or individuals.

Frail is our vessel, and the ocean is wide;
but as in your mercy you have set our course,
so steer the vessel of our life
towards the everlasting shore of peace,
and bring us at length
to the quiet haven of our heart's desire,
where you, O God,
are blessed, and live and reign
for ever and ever.
Amen.

MUSIC IN PRAYER

Although it never fit into the genre of "spiritual" music, John Stewart's song "Botswana" was a favorite for my husband, children, and me. The lyrics speak of the unease the songwriter has in living in an upscale part of Los Angeles when there are so many social injustices taking place across the world. Thus, he laments "the pictures of the children with the flies in their eyes" and wonders if God cries at such a sight. It provoked many discussions for us over the years.

Using music for prayer fits more naturally into some families than others. Quiet music can be used as a backdrop for family litanies or reflections. Singing simple responses, such as those used at church, offers a different way to pray. Or a song like "Botswana" generates prayers for those in need.

Singing the grace before meals is another way to incorporate music into a family ritual. The following prayer is sung to the tune of "Edelweiss" from "The Sound of Music."

Bless our friends,
Bless our food,
Come, O Lord and sit with us.

May our talk
Glow with peace;
Come with your love to surround us.

Friendship and love
May they bloom and glow,
Bloom and glow forever.

Bless our friends,
Bless our food,
Bless all people forever.

➤ **SOURCE UNKNOWN**

SINGING IN CHURCH

Most young children love to sing. Thus, it is a frustration when the music at church is either uninteresting or too complex for participation by children. The following suggestions might help children take a more active part in liturgies and prayer services at church:

- Encourage them to sing in "spurts." Examples of this would be the psalm refrain, the acclamations before the readings from the lectionary, refrains from hymns, and those parts of the liturgy that are sung each week, such as the "Holy, Holy."
- Check with your child's catechist or teacher about the music used in religious education classes. If available, purchase a CD of the songs used in your child's class and use it as a prayer resource for your family.
- Use music as a meditative prayer. Classical pieces lend themselves to this as well as Gregorian chant and the music from Taizé.
- Encourage older children and adolescents to create a mix of their personal "spirituals"—those songs that express longing, joy, reverence, praise, and thanksgiving for and to God.

Gestures in Prayer

The church has a long tradition of using gesture in prayer. During worship, we genuflect, cross ourselves, bow our heads, kneel, sit, and stand. Through body language, each of these bring a particular mood or meaning to our prayers. Teaching children these gestures heightens their consciousness around prayer and fosters a reverence for God and for the act of praying. Here are some gestures that can be incorporated into a family's prayer life:

- The Sign of the Cross to begin and end prayers of grace and blessing
- Folding the hands when offering a prayer out loud or praying quietly
- Bowing the head when offering grace at meals or when offer-

ing prayers of intercession or petition

- Hugging one another when finishing a prayer of blessing or thanksgiving
- Crossing the arms over the chest when offering prayers of forgiveness and for peace
- Kneeling when saying prayers at bedtime
- Holding hands when offering grace or blessing an object, such as the Christmas tree (see Chapter 3)
- Raising the arms when offering prayers of praise

Gestures can easily be fitted to this prayer that dates back to the eleventh century. It is a good prayer for starting the day, or in times of decision making.

God be in my head,
    And in my understanding;
God be in my eyes,
    And in my looking;
God be in my mouth,
    And in my speaking;
God be in my heart,
    And in my thinking;
God be at my end,
    And at my departing.
— **Sarum Primer**

Meditation in Prayer
"Be still, and know that I am God!" — **Psalm 46:10**

If using words and talking to God comes easily, listening is a bit more challenging, especially in the midst of a busy household. The practice of meditation entails periods of silence in which we make a concerted effort to seek a greater understanding of God and of our faith. Sustained attentiveness is even difficult in a monastery, so we needn't worry if we can't perfect it in the living room. Reading a short passage from the Bible or a book on spirituality helps to focus and to let our minds settle. Such practices lift us up and away from daily distractions, and offer something better to think about than crazy schedules or what's on TV. This makes meditation a welcome respite for every family.

Prayer Beads

Prayer beads have been used for centuries by Christians, Muslims, Buddhists, Sikhs, and others. The act of meditating with a circle of beads worn on the wrist or passing through the fingers is a calming experience that is partnered with reflection. What's more, this practice of meditation can be done with others as well as in solitude. Here are some uses of prayer beads that can be incorporated into family prayer:

- The Catholic Rosary consists of five sets of ten beads, or decades, along with a crucifix and four additional beads. The prayer begins with the Sign of the Cross and then the Apostle's Creed. An Our Father is offered, followed by three Hail Marys and one Glory to the Father. To pray the decades, begin with an Our Father on the larger bead and then ten Hail Marys. The Glory to the Father ends each decade. The repetition of these prayers allows for meditation on the lives of Jesus and Mary. These are called the Mysteries of the Rosary and include the Joyful Mysteries, the Sorrowful Mysteries, the Glorious Mysteries, and the Mysteries of Light. Variations on these meditations, such as one centered on justice and peace, can be found through web and print resources.

- The Anglican Rosary is made up of thirty-three beads, one for each year of Jesus' life. A larger bead is placed at the start of each of four sets of seven smaller beads (called "weeks"). A cross and two large beads provide a starting point for the prayer and begin with the Sign of the Cross and an Our Father. Unlike the Catholic Rosary, there are no set prayers for the Anglican Rosary. One might choose the Jesus Prayer (see Chapter 1), the Serenity Prayer, a verse from the psalms, or another short prayer to repeat on each of the small (cruciform) beads and another one for the larger (invitatory) beads. The circle of beads is prayed three times, to symbolize the Holy Trinity. The slow and rhythmic pace of the prayer makes it a meditative practice for an individual or family.

Lectio Divina

Another type of meditation is called *Lectio Divina*, which means "divine reading." It is a way to use Scripture that speaks to the heart and invites a prayerful response. Here is how a family might use *Lectio Divina*:

- Choose a gospel story that is appropriate to the age and comprehension level of your child.

- Read the passage slowly. Invite family members to share a word or a phrase that stands out for them.
- Read the passage again. Try to imagine being part of the scene. What would you talk to Jesus about?
- Sit quietly and think about the words from the Bible and what they mean to you. Invite each family member to choose one word that reminds them of God's love.
- Talk about ways to respond to what you have heard by doing something that will show God's love in your lives over the next day or week.
- Close with a favorite prayer.

Lectio Divina Scriptures for a Family

MARK 10:46–52
The healing of blind Bartimaeus

LUKE 15:3–7
The parable of the lost sheep

MATTHEW 19:13–14
Jesus blesses little children

LUKE 11:33-36
Let your light shine

MARK 8:1-10
Feeding the four thousand

Praying with Art and Images

Icons are a revered tradition in the Eastern Orthodox tradition and might be considered doorways to the sacred. Father Bill McNichols, a renowned iconographer, describes them as bringing one into the presence of holy people and inviting conversation with them in the midst of ordinary life.

Throughout the centuries, artwork has opened up insight and imagination through the depiction of religious themes. Some of this served a practical purpose as well as an aesthetic one. Stained glass windows, for example, were often used to help people who had no access to books or formal education learn about the teachings of the church, the events of the Bible, and the lives of the saints. Families can draw upon art as a way to engage in prayer that is reflective and meditative, as well as interactive and lively. Visits to art galleries and churches provide access to classical as well as modern art.

> *The purpose of the icons and images is to bring you into the presence of each Heavenly individual and to allow you to gaze upon them while conversing with them during your prayers in daily life.*
>
> — **FATHER BILL McNICHOLS**

Art does not need to be explicitly religious to be spiritual. Paintings or photographs of natural landscapes awaken an appreciation for the beauty of nature. Sculpture generates an appreciation for the wondrous working of the human body. Whatever form it takes, artwork can be used to focus attention during family prayer or serve as a backdrop to a "domestic shrine" (see Chapter 4).

The Painting That Inspired Henri Nouwen

Rembrandt's painting "The Return of the Prodigal Son" so moved the late Henri Nouwen that he traveled all the way to Saint Petersburg, Russia, to contemplate it. Nouwen, a Dutch priest, is considered by many to be one of the most influential spiritual voices of our time. His visit to the Hermitage gallery involved sitting before the painting for hours so that he could take in every

detail of the tender embrace of father and son. Nouwen
went on to write about both the painting and the par-
able that inspired it in a stunning book about forgive-
ness and God's infinite mercy. Since the setting for both
the story and the painting takes place within the family,
it is a beautiful example of life inspiring art.

Contemplation in Prayer

Take my yoke upon you, and learn from me; for I am gentle and
humble in heart, and you will find rest for your souls.

⟹ **Matthew11:29**

In her book *Dance of the Spirit*, the late Maria Harris used the
example of two mothers, one pregnant and the other nursing
her baby, to illustrate the practice of contemplation. Each one
has achieved a state of stillness without being conscious of it.
Through the experience of motherhood they are both in touch
with the Divine Mystery.

There is a Hasidic saying that goes, *"Behind every blade of grass*
stands an angel telling it to grow." It's an image that speaks of the
wondrous nature of life, one that can pass us by if we don't stop
now and then to pay attention. Jesus' invitation to follow him was
one toward rest and the discovery of gentleness and humility.
What a far cry from the media messages we receive on a regular
basis that tell us to do, to have, and to want more.

Thomas Merton was a Trappist monk widely known for his
prolific writing on spirituality. He defined contemplation as a
"loving sense of this life and this presence and this eternity." It

is the ultimate way of remaining in the *now*. Rather than being attainable only for monks and nuns, however, contemplation is an expression of prayer that can be beautifully woven into the fabric of family life. It calls for the cultivation of attentiveness to where we are and what we are doing. As such, it provides a way to pray without words, cultivating what Saint Thérèse of Lisieux called "a surge of the heart." It offers a respite from the demands of daily life and responsibility. And it opens up a vision that enables us to see angels in the backyard and God's smile twinkling in a child's eyes.

The Gift of Silence and Solitude

Nature Deficit Disorder (see Chapter 1) is caused not only by a lack of exposure to the outdoors but also by the absence of silence. Joggers, bicyclists, hikers, and others who seem to be enjoying the beauty of nature are often plugged into something that feeds music or motivational messages into their ears. Continual noise is breaking down our natural attention to the sounds of nature and even to the dangers posed by predators or moving vehicles.

The danger to the soul may run deeper. When offering retreats and talks to parents and teachers, I often caution them against the overuse of "time-outs" with kids. By using silence and solitude to punish children, we relay a message that two of our most time-honored spiritual traditions are wrong!

When I was teaching in a Catholic school, I used to take the children in my second-grade class to the empty church on occasion and let them wander around. They loved the chance to explore the environment and to satisfy their curiosity about the different symbols and furnishings that they rarely saw up close. At one point, I would invite all of them to find a space of their own in which to sit and be still. They loved it.

It's best to introduce children to silence and solitude as contemplative practices in incremental ways. Here are some ideas:

- Rather than impose either one on a child, model its benefits. Take time on a regular basis for your own quiet time. Use it to read a book, write in a journal, or pray. By teaching children to respect the parameters of a parent's need for quiet and rest, we let them know how beneficial these times are.

> *Contemplation means gazing at something with an uncluttered view, being as wide-awake as possible, and attempting to be as free from preoccupation and preconception as we can.* — **MARIA HARRIS**

- Allow children to play by themselves without constantly interrupting or talking to them. Set a time each day to shut off the television and computer and to encourage each family member to have time alone. Make sure young children are in a place where they are safe and "in view" without being intrusive.

- Take a family trip to a church, shrine, or retreat center where silence is valued. Even a cemetery is a great place for being still. Encourage them to immerse themselves in the beauty of silence. Have an honest conversation about what makes it hard to be quiet or to be alone, or both.

Reflection on Psalm 46:10

Here is a popular meditation technique that can be used to quiet the mind and make it receptive for quiet prayer. Read the psalm passage and then drop off words until you reach the first one. Breathe slowly in and out as you say the words. Each time, be aware of sinking deeper into silence and a quieting of the mind. This is a good exercise to teach children as a way to introduce them to the benefits of silent prayer and contemplation.

> *Be still, and know that I am God!*
> *Be still and know that I am...*
> *Be still...*
> *Be...*

Learning to Listen

Listen with the ear of your heart. ⟹ **SAINT BENEDICT**

It's hard to listen to God, if we can't first listen to one another. Here are five habits for cultivating a listening ear that will, in time, lead to a listening heart:

1. Stop talking—resist the urge to interrupt or change the subject.
2. Eliminate distractions— turn off the television or computer; stop fiddling with things or working on

A Wise Old Owl

A wise old owl
Sat in an oak
The more he heard
The less he spoke
The less he spoke
The more he heard
Why can't we all
Be like that wise old bird?

⟹ **NURSERY RHYME,**
SOURCE UNKNOWN

something; give your full attention to listening.

3. Focus on the speaker—maintain eye contact and ask questions to make sure you understand what is being said.

4. Listen beneath the words—body language and "meta-messages" are other ways to listen. What may be left unsaid starts to emerge when we are really paying attention to the speaker.

5. Show appreciation—thank the speaker for being honest and open. Share what a gift it is to listen to one another.

Prayers and Rituals for the Home

CHAPTER 3

WHEN
to pray

t's sometimes said that the only person who prays well is the one who prays often. If prayer is understood, however, as something undertaken only during times of quiet and calm, then family life is the last place to find it. The good news is that prayer is easily folded into the rhythm of our days, weeks, months, and years, no matter how offbeat these times might be. Although it may not solve the problem of overstuffed schedules, prayer helps us shape the time we have been given.

In his book *Pray All Ways*, Father Edward Hays describes how Jesus calls us into a living communion with God. To do so means threading prayer into each day as well as the seasons of both nature and worship. Jesus is an ideal model for such prayer. As a faithful Jew, he observed the prayers of his people through the marking of holy days and festivals. Thus, he prayed in the synagogue and temple and at the Passover meal that we call the Last Supper. He prayed before sharing food with others and before performing miracles and healings. He prayed during his hour of agony in the Garden of Gethsemane and his solitary time in the desert. And, in an especially heartening message for those

> *The different activities of our daily lives are not distractions from prayer but rather the rich soil for prayer.* ⸺ **Edward Hays**

with busy lives, he said that prayers needn't be long or formal. Simply "show up," as one contemplative puts it, and you will find God waiting to listen.

Until we learn to pray always and in all ways, says Fr. Hays, we are in danger of replacing prayer with busyness and even with "small acts of kindness." The tasks that we undertake and the service we provide to others are certainly important, but if they are separated from a prayerful heart, they can grow empty and fruitless. The great German mystic Hildegard of Bingen once noted that there was nothing sadder than a drooping soul. The only way to keep it alive and vibrant is by watering it regularly with the replenishing waters of prayer.

DAILY PRAYER
By day the Lord commands his steadfast love, and at night his song is with me, a prayer to the God of my life. ⸺ **Psalm 42:8**

Praying throughout the day is a regular practice among

Christians, Jews, and Muslims. The daily cycle, set in place by the rising and setting of the sun, contains particular "hours" for prayer. This ancient practice is referenced in Psalm 119:164: *"Seven times a day I praise you...."* Early Christians marked these times of prayer at dawn (*prime* or first hour), nine AM (*terce* or third hour), noon (*sext* or sixth hour), three PM (*none* or ninth hour), six PM (*vespers* or evening hour), and night (*compline* or the hour of retiring). (Vigils, or *Matins*, forms an eighth "hour," that of keeping the night watch.) Over the centuries the church compressed these into four—morning (*lauds*), noon, vespers, and compline. Christians of both Eastern and Western traditions celebrate the "Liturgy of the Hours" under different names and with slight variations.

Many of us might long for someone to ring a bell that summons us to periods of quiet and provides a break from busyness and fatigue. Although not triggered by bell-tolling, there is a rhythm to domestic life that contains natural stopping points throughout the day. We might call these the Liturgy of Family Hours.

Morning Prayer

O Lord, open my lips, and my mouth shall declare your praise.

➡ PSALM 51:15

This is the psalm that, as part of the Liturgy of the Hours, begins each offering of Morning Prayer. They are fitting words with which to start each day. Traditionally the Sign of the Cross is traced on the lips as this psalm is said. It's a simple practice to teach children.

Morning is a good time for prayers of petition. We arise with a sense of anticipation or reluctance, depending on what lies ahead of us that day. The prayers we offer, whether by ourselves or as a family, can set a positive tone and a thoughtful rhythm for the hours that will follow.

Prayers of oblation offer everything we have to God. Morning is an opportune time for such prayer. In the midst of thoughts and plans that lie ahead of us in the day's activities, we can also give ourselves into God's hands. Such prayer often bounces back to us as we move through the tasks and responsibilities that engage us. Reminders of a morning offering might help us move a little slower or take extra effort in tending to another's needs. It can also inspire us to give over to God anything we feel unable or unwilling to handle.

Morning Offering

O Lord, you know what is best for me. Let me conduct myself according to your pleasure. Give me what you will, how much you will, and when you will. Set me where you will and deal with me as you think best. Behold, I am your servant, prepared for anything, for I desire not to live for myself but for you. May I do so worthily and perfectly. ⮕ THOMAS A KEMPIS

Noon Prayer

Have you ever heard a bell ringing at noon? The practice started in the 15th century when Pope Calixtus III asked for a midday ringing of bells and prayers for protection against the Turkish invasions of the time. Many churches continue the practice, sometimes by playing hymns sounded out with electronic bell tones.

In some countries, noon is a time of *siesta*, or a midday nap. The word itself is Spanish and is derived from the Latin "sext"—the noonday prayer. While few of us enjoy the luxury of a nap, the call to pause and find a midday resting point is a nice way to appreciate the bounty of God. When packing a lunch

> *Blessed are you, Lord God, who brings forth the fruit of the earth.*
>
> ➤ **JEWISH MEALTIME PRAYER**

for a child (or themselves), parents might slip a short prayer or tip for taking a "joy break" inside. Here are some suggestions:

- An affirmation or message of affection
- A verse from a favorite psalm
- A word of thanks for something the child did or said
- A reminder about something fun the family did together
- A mealtime prayer or a prayer for peace

Evening Prayer

For families, evening rituals of returning home, preparing dinner, and sitting around a table can be loaded with stress and strain. Gathering for a meal is often a challenge and yet, as research shows, families who do so are healthier as a result. Table time offers an opportunity for rituals of thanksgiving and blessing. When parents safeguard this time, the evening hour is shaped into something happy and holy.

Mealtime blessings, or "grace," can vary from traditional prayers to spontaneous ones. They can also be offered in a number of ways. Here are just a few:

- Assign each family member a different night of the week to choose the blessing of his or her choice.
- Do a round-robin grace by naming something for which to give thanks and praise.
- Put the prayer to music and sing the grace together (see Chapter 1 for an example).
- Take a moment of silence before offering the prayer and then offer a traditional mealtime blessing.
- Vary the list of blessings around food each night by including: those who prepared the meal, the food itself and how it will nurture the family, the enjoyment of the family as they share the meal, those who are hungry and without food, those whose labor brought the food to the table.
- Alternate verses of a traditional mealtime blessing.
- Stand around the table, hold hands, bow your heads, or use other gestures as part of the prayer.
- Use a psalm such as 145:15–16—*"The eyes of all look to you, and you give them their food in due season. You open your hand, satisfying the desire of every living thing."*

Night Prayer

Night prayers offer opportunities to quiet the mind and ready ourselves for sleep. In addition to providing parents time to bless their child, these prayers bring us to the end of a day in peace. Thus, the offering of night prayer is a valuable ritual for parents. The following prayers are examples of the letting go that is folded into prayer at the end of the day.

A Blessing at Evening

Most Loving God, Light within the Heavens,
as we come to our rest this night we entrust ourselves
*   into Your care.*
Grant that we may rest
*   securely in Your Spirit*
and make each breath an
*   offering even as we sleep.*

Quiet the storms that may
*   be in our hearts.*
Cradle us in Your tender
*   embrace and*
keep within our inward ears
*   Your eternal pulse.*
May we rock gently in You
*   as a boat upon the evening*
*   waters.*

Guard our dreaming
*   and even there keep all*
*   anxiety at bay.*
May the shortcomings
*   and cares of this day*
*   be swept away*
in a tide of renewing rest that we may wake ready to
seek Your face at daybreak and to travel another day
*   in Your Love. Amen.*

> **KEN PHILLIPS. USED WITH PERMISSION**

Prayer at the End of a Busy Day

Eternal God,
It's been a long day.
As we settle down
*   for the night,*
bring peace to our home.
Grant us a restful night.
Help us to leave behind
*   the day's activities.*
Awaken us in the morning
*   with energy for*
*   a new day.*
In gratitude for the gift
*   of sleep, we pray.*
Amen.

> **ADAPTED FROM POCKET PRAYERS FOR PARENTS**

In Chapter 1, I noted how bedtime blessings provide wonderful one-on-one time with a child. It is also an ideal time to teach children simple prayers and encourage them to nurture a prayer life of their own. Several years ago, I came across a clever ritual called a "prayer rock." It consists of wrapping a small stone in a piece of fabric and tying it with a ribbon. The corresponding verse reminds children to make prayer a part of their nightly routine and again in the morning. I am unsure of the author of this poem, but I'm grateful for its sweet images and gentle reminders to pray both night and day.

I'm your little prayer rock and this is what I'll do.
Just put me on your pillow till the day is through.
Then turn back the covers and climb into your bed
And WHACK...your little prayer rock will hit you on your head.
Then you will remember as the day is through
To kneel and say your prayers as you wanted to.
Then when you are finished just dump me on the floor,
I'll stay there through the nighttime to give you help once more.
When you get up in the morning, CLUNK...I'll stub your toe
So you will remember your prayers before you go.
Put me on your pillow when your bed is made,
And your clever little prayer rock will continue in your aid.
Because your heavenly Father cares and loves you so,
He wants you to remember to talk to him, you know.

Seasonal Prayer

"You have made the moon to mark the seasons; the sun knows its time for setting." ⹀ Psalm 104:19

As commonplace as calendars are today, it was not always so. At one time, the practice of looking into the future was considered too sacred for ordinary people. Thus, calendars were reserved for priests and shamans—those deemed holy enough to make wise use of their powers.

While most secular calendars are linear, the church year is often depicted in the round. This reflects its cyclic and repetitive characteristics, ones filled with rituals, symbols, and stories. Liturgical seasons are marked off and shaded with corresponding symbolic colors. Each one contains particular feasts that celebrate the story of Christ's life, ministry, passion, death, Resurrection, and Ascension into heaven. While modern culture has secularized many of these holy days with symbols such as Santa Claus and the Easter Bunny, their spiritual meanings can and should prevail.

Celebrating the church year opens up an array of ways for families to pray. Beginning with the season of Advent and moving through Christmas, Lent, Easter, and the weeks dubbed "Ordinary Time," the liturgical calendar provides a rich framework for connecting religious rituals with those of domestic life.

In like manner, making connections with the natural seasons of the year is one of the most effective ways to tie prayer and ritual with the cycles of family life. Perhaps the people in ancient times were onto something when they saw the keeping of calendars as a sacred practice. Doing so in ritualistic fashion reminds us again and again of the sanctity of time as the sun and moon mark each day and move us through the months of the year.

PRAYING THROUGH THE CHURCH YEAR

"This day shall be a day of remembrance for you. You shall celebrate it as a festival to the Lord; through your generations you shall observe it as a perpetual ordinance." — EXODUS 12:14

The church year begins with the First Sunday of Advent and concludes with the feast of Christ the King. Since entire books have been written about each season and holy day, the following ideas are just a sample of what families can do to celebrate each one.

Rituals of Advent

Advent, the four weeks (counted by Sundays) prior to Christmas, marks the festival celebration of Christ's birth in history as well as his coming at the end of the world. It is a season of preparation, waiting, and anticipation. Coinciding in the northern hemisphere with the winter solstice, the season also tracks the movement out of darkness and into light. It is a busy time of year for families as well as one rich in customs and traditions. There is much that parents can do to keep the commercial aspects of the holidays from overshadowing the spiritual significance of this time of year.

The Advent Wreath

The ritual of the Advent Wreath first began in the home and was gradually drawn into church worship. The wreath is made up of four candles—three purple or blue and one pink—set within a circle of evergreen branches. Each week of Advent, another candle on the wreath is lit, accompanied by prayer. The multiplication of light that comes with the sequential lighting of candles makes this an especially engaging ritual for children. Take prayers for each of the weeks of Advent from print or web resources, or make up your own. Here is a simple one that is especially appropriate for young children:

Jesus,
Be with us as we light a candle on the Advent wreath.
Let your light fill our home.
Give us loving and joyful hearts as we await your coming.
Amen.

The O Antiphons

During the eight days before Christmas, the O Antiphons are chanted as a way to prepare for the coming of Jesus. Each one begins with a title for Christ. The antiphons provide a great antidote to consumerism as well as opportunities for reflection about the meaning of Christmas. They can also encourage us to put Christ-like behaviors and attitudes into practice. Here are the antiphons and reflections to go with each one:

- December 17—O *Wisdom of our God Most High, guiding creation with power and love: come to teach us the path of knowledge.* Ask God for guidance in making good choices about what to eat, drink, shop for, and do during the holidays.
- December 18—O *Leader of the House of Israel, giver of the Law to Moses on Sinai: come to rescue us with your mighty power.*

Reflect on the ways God has "rescued" your family with love and grace during the past year.

- December 19—*O Root of Jesse's stem, sign of God's love for all his people: come to save us without delay!* Jesus brings hope, especially to those who are poor or suffering. Offer a prayer for those in need today.
- December 20—*O Key of David, opening the gates of God's eternal Kingdom: come and free the prisoners of darkness.* When we hurt one another through careless actions or cruel words, we are truly cast into darkness. Pray for the light of forgiveness today.
- December 21—*O Rising Dawn, splendor of eternal light, sun of justice: come and shine on those who dwell in darkness and in the shadow of death.* In the Northern Hemisphere, the winter solstice marks the longest night of the year. Give praise to God for the beauty of morning light.
- December 22—*O King of nations and keystone of the Church: come and save humankind, whom you formed from the dust!* Pray today for all nations of the world and for a restoration of peace among them.
- December 23—*O Emmanuel, our King and Giver of Law: come to save us, Lord our God!* Christmas is just two days away. Share with one another what you are hoping for this Christmas and pray for a joyful celebration of this great feast.

Christmas Traditions, Symbols, and Blessings

There may be no other time of the year so full of symbols and traditions than Christmas. Many of these are secular but have their roots in the religious significance of the season. Parents can strengthen the link between them by creating rituals of blessings around them.

Santa Claus and Saint Nicholas

One of the most challenging traditions connected to Christmas is the character of Santa Claus. This figure has gone through a major metamorphosis since its origins in Saint Nicholas, the kindly bishop who brought gifts to poor children. Other traditions particular to various countries, such as Father Christmas, are also connected with Santa Claus. A child's belief in Santa Claus is relatively harmless if parents keep a reign on the consumerism that has become tied to him. Three ways to counter this and to bring a spiritual element back into the season include:

- Celebrating the Feast of Saint Nicholas on December 6 with a blessing of candy canes and sharing of simple treats.

> **Other Ideas for Christmas Blessings**
>
> *Bless the stockings as you hang them in place.*
>
> *Bless the ingredients for special recipes you are preparing for Christmas meals.*
>
> *Bless the rooms where houseguests will be sleeping.*

- Taking part in Christmas projects at your parish and involving children in shopping for, wrapping, and bringing gifts to families with limited resources.
- Emphasizing the importance of generosity and gratitude at this time of year, particularly with regard to giving and receiving presents.

The Christmas Tree

Decorating the Christmas tree is often an occasion for storytelling as memories surface around the ornaments and where they originated. It's also an opportunity for sharing prayers of blessing—for the tree and its decorations, as well as for the gifts that are placed beneath it.

Blessing of the Christmas Tree

Be with us as we gather around this tree, Jesus.
Let its twinkling lights and glittering ornaments
remind us of the brightness of your love.
Bless us all as we share the gifts we have for one another,
and the great gift that comes through you.
Amen.

The Nativity Scene (Crèche)

Tradition has it that Saint Francis of Assisi popularized the manger scene by using people and live animals to re-create the night of Jesus' birth. Gathering around the crèche can be accompanied by a reading of the Nativity accounts .

- The foretelling of Jesus' birth to Mary by an angel—Luke 1:26–38
- Mary's visit to her cousin Elizabeth—Luke 1:39–56
- The Birth of Jesus—Luke 2:1–7
- The shepherds and angels—Luke 2:8–20
- The visit of the Magi—Matthew 2:1–12
- The flight into Egypt—Matthew 2:13–15

Blessing of the Crèche

Jesus,
You were born into a loving family, and visited
by angels and animals, shepherds and kings.
Bless us as we place each
figure into the manger scene.
May our love for you and one another grow
as we celebrate the wonder of your birth.
Amen.

Rituals of Lent

Lent is the forty-day preparation prior to the feast and season of Easter. Three traditional practices are emphasized during this time—prayer, penance, and almsgiving. Lent was originally a time of preparation for those who were to be baptized at Easter. The root of our English word "Lent" means "springtime." It is a season that readies us all for the glorious celebration of Christ's Resurrection from the dead as new life emerges all around us.

The Practice of Prayer

All seasons are times for prayer, but lenten prayer has special significance. Prayers of petition (especially for forgiveness) and meditation are particularly fitting for a season of repentance and reflection.

Ash Wednesday Ashes have traditionally been associated with being a penitent—one seeking forgiveness for sins and restoration with the faith community. The ritual on Ash Wednesday in which we are marked on the forehead with a cross of ashes is more of an encouragement to return to God than a chastisement for our failings. Thus, the words of the ritual, *"Turn away from sin and be faithful to the gospel"* (Mark 1:15), are a reminder to place our priorities in right order. As families move into Lent, they can continue to use this simple phrase as part of a mealtime blessing or nightly prayer, accompanied by the Sign of the Cross. It can also lead to discussions about ways we remain "turned toward God" in our everyday lives.

The Stations of the Cross One of the most cherished traditions during Lent is praying the Stations of the Cross. Originally undertaken as part of a pilgrimage to the Holy Land, the *Via Dolorosa*, or Way of Sorrows, follows Jesus from his sentence of execution by Pilate to the removal of his lifeless body from the cross. There are fourteen stations (some versions add a fifteenth for the Resurrection) where pilgrims pause to pray and reflect on the meaning of Christ's passion and death. The Stations can be prayed with others in a parish or other religious setting, or by oneself. Online versions are available, but it is much more engaging for families to physically walk the prayer together.

> *We adore you, O Christ,*
> *and we praise you.*
> *Because by your holy cross*
> *you have redeemed*
> *the world.*
>
> ⸺ TRADITIONAL PRAYER AND
> RESPONSE FOR THE STATIONS
> OF THE CROSS

The Practice of Penance

"But when you fast, put oil on your head and wash your face, so that your fasting may be seen not by others but by your Father

who is in secret; and your
Father who sees in secret will
reward you." — MATTHEW 6:17–18

Fasting in the Family Fasting
and abstinence—refraining from
quantities and kinds of food—
are historical lenten practices
that are still emphasized today.

> **A Penitential Psalm for Lent**
> Have mercy on me,
> O God; according to
> your steadfast love;
> according to your
> abundant mercy blot
> out my transgressions.

Catholics abstain from eating meat on Ash Wednesday and each
Friday during Lent, and eat one main meal on Ash Wednesday
and Good Friday. These penitential acts take on enriched meaning in families when we learn to fast or abstain from certain
behaviors and attitudes. Here are some suggestions that might
trigger other ideas for your family:

- Fast from too much "screen time" by turning off televisions
  and computers for an extra hour each day.
- Abstain from complaining, and look for ways to affirm one
  another.
- Fast from overload by cutting down on outside activities and
  seeking time together as a family.
- Abstain from stubbornness and being opinionated, and look
  for ways to seek and extend forgiveness and understanding to
  other family members.
- Fast from unhealthy practices, such as indulging in too much
  sugar or junk food, and focus on eating healthy, nutritious
  foods.
- Abstain from criticizing or judging others, and pay attention
  to their good qualities instead.

Giving to Those in Need

Like the other traditional lenten practices, taking care of the poor is a year-round priority. During the lenten season, the practice of "almsgiving" might be coupled with that of "spring cleaning." Not only might we simplify our own lives, but we can cultivate empathy and compassion for those who have so little.

Parishes often have special collections of clothing, food, and other items for homeless shelters and food banks. Engage the entire family in deciding on donations and assembling the items. Make it into a simple ritual by offering prayers of intercession for those to whom the donations will be given.

Rituals of Triduum

The celebration of the Triduum—the "Three Days"—is the most sacred time on the church calendar. Participating in your parish liturgies is the best possible way to immerse yourself in the rituals, symbols, and prayers that surround the account of Jesus' passion, death, and Resurrection. In addition, there are ways to make connections between the home and the church through simple family rituals and prayers.

Holy Thursday

One of the rituals enacted during the Holy Thursday liturgy is the washing of feet. This humble gesture follows the example of Jesus, who washed the feet of his disciples to show them how to serve one another. In similar fashion, family members might perform a specific act of service at some point during the day and then discuss what it takes to be a humble servant of God.

Place a special emphasis on the mealtime blessing as you recall how Jesus shared a final meal with his friends.

Good Friday

A liturgical tradition performed on Good Friday is the veneration of the cross. After the reading of the passion, worshippers come forward to kiss, or kneel or bow before, the cross. This sign of respect and adoration is a profound way to honor Christ. Families might place a cross or crucifix in a prominent place on this day. Gather around it to offer prayers of intercession for those who carry heavy crosses in life, such as illness, grief, alienation from loved ones, or the terrors of war.

Holy Saturday

The Easter Vigil is a magnificent liturgy that takes place on the evening of Holy Saturday. This sacred celebration begins in darkness, which is pierced by the igniting of a fire and the lighting of the Easter candle. After the candle is carried in procession into the church, the deacon or priest sings the "Exultet," or Easter Proclamation. The long period of preparation for Easter is over. The light of Christ shines in our midst.

In similar fashion, families might buy a white candle for use throughout the Easter season. Each time it is lit, use the Easter Proclamation and offer prayers of praise and thanksgiving for the gifts of life and light. In addition, offer prayers of intercession for those who were baptized or received into the church during the Easter Vigil.

Rituals of Easter

Like Christmas, Easter is both a feast day and a season. When Lent began, we heard the story of Jesus being drawn into the desert, where he fasted and prayed. On Easter Sunday, we hear the account of his emergence from a tomb of death and into a garden of life. Churches are filled with symbols of new life— white cloths and vestments that replace the somber purple of

> **The Easter Proclamation**
>
> *Light of Christ!*
> *Thanks be to God!*

Lent; lilies and other flowers; bells and the return of the "Alleluia," which has been silenced for six weeks. It's a joyous celebration.

As your family prepares for and celebrates Easter, keep in mind these death-to-life images. Each is present in traditional Easter customs:

- Coloring Easter eggs—symbolic of spring as well as the tomb from which Jesus emerged
- New clothes—symbolic of the white garment that is part of the baptismal service and being "clothed in Christ" (Galatians 3:27)
- Lamb—symbolic of Jesus, the Lamb of God
- Easter Bunny—symbolic of fertility and the abundance of new life
- Butterflies—symbolic of the stages of the life of Christ from caterpillar (earthly life), cocoon (death and dormancy in the tomb), and butterfly (rising to new, transformed life)

Easter Gardens

Nothing is more symbolic of new life than a garden in the spring. As buds emerge and flowers bloom, we witness anew the abundance of God's creation. Whether you have a plot of ground or simply an empty pot, planting seeds is a wonderful way to mark the season of Easter. Offer prayers of blessing after planting seeds and each time they are watered. Prayers of thanksgiving and praise come naturally as leaves, flowers, fruits, or vegetables begin to grow.

A visit to a botanical or community garden is another lovely way to keep the season holy. Check online for a list of "quiet gardens" through the movement of the same name. These gardens are grown throughout the world as places of refuge and prayer.

A Garden Prayer

Oh Lord Jesus,
*   true gardener,*
work in us what you want
*   of us.*
For you are indeed
*   the true gardener,*
at once, maker and tiller
*   and keeper of your*
*   garden.*
You who plant
*   with the word,*
water with the spirit,
and give your increase
*   and your power.*
— **GUERRIC OF IGNY,**
12TH CENTURY

Rituals of Pentecost

The Easter season ends with another festive celebration. The account of the first Pentecost describes how the Holy Spirit comes in the midst of a violent wind as the disciples are gathered together. *"Divided tongues, as of fire, appeared among them, and a tongue rested on each of them."* Empowered by the Spirit, they then testify to their faith in various languages to the diverse crowd who assembles at the sound of the wind (Acts 2:1–13).

It's hard to think of a more dramatic scene.

Praying to the Holy Spirit for wisdom, understanding, and inspiration is especially helpful during times of transition or discernment, or when we just need a boost of morale. Coinciding, as it

> **A Prayer for Guidance**
>
> *May the Spirit give us*
> *light to guide us,*
> *courage to support us,*
> *and love to unite us,*
> *now and evermore.*
>
> ➡ **SOURCE UNKNOWN**

does, with graduations and end-of-the-school-year activities, Pentecost reminds us to open ourselves to the guidance and grace of the Holy Spirit whenever we are facing changes in our lives. This is especially helpful for families because of the way a change in the life of one family member ripples throughout the household. While we may not be visited by wind and fire, the gentle prodding of God's Spirit can move us out of inertia and into positive action.

Rituals for Secular Holidays

In addition to the lovely opportunities for prayer and ritual during the liturgical seasons, there are a number of secular holidays that are particularly meaningful for families.

New Year's Day

The revelry that accompanies the ringing in of a new year speaks strongly to hope for a more promising future. For families, the holiday provides a window for looking back on the past year and ahead to what the new year might bring. Make this into a ritual by using a calendar to recall the highlights of the previous year, particularly the blessings received. Then make a hope list for the year to come. Place the list in a place where you will remember to read it next New Year's. Offer a spontaneous prayer of thanksgiving for God's many blessings.

Valentine's Day

Prayers of adoration are simply love songs to God. No one was better at expressing these than the mystics—those saints and holy people who recognized God's love in every detail of their daily lives. Their prayers rang with adoration for God while also recognizing God's immeasurable love for us.

One of the most eloquent of these mystics was Julian of Norwich, who lived a secluded life in the 14th century. After surviving a major illness, she recorded a number of visions, or "showings," which revealed to her the unconditional love of God. Follow her example of looking for Divine love by writing a family valentine for God. Decorate it as desired and keep it in a special place for the entire week as a reminder of God's unending love.

A Vision of God's Love

No mere creature
*   can ever imagine*
just how dearly, sweetly,
*   and tenderly*
our Creator loves us.
So with his grace and aid,
let us spiritually rest
*   in contemplation,*
forever marveling
at the high, surpassing,
*   single-minded,*
immeasurable love
that our good Lord
*   extends to us.*
⇒ JULIAN OF NORWICH

Dominion Day and Independence Day

Coming, as they do, in the middle of summer, the celebrations of Dominion Day (July 1) in Canada and Independence Day (July 4) in the United States are great times to be outdoors enjoying friends and fireworks, picnics and parades. Seize the opportunity to offer thanksgiving for the gift of freedom, and to pray on behalf of those who are enslaved, imprisoned, or oppressed.

In Thanksgiving for Freedom

Saving God,
Thank you for the freedoms we enjoy.
May we never take them for granted.
Thank you for the blessings of our land and our people.
May we grow strong in our dedication to justice and
  compassion.
Thank you for the work and sacrifice of others that made our
  country great.
May we continue their efforts through a commitment to justice
  and peace.
Bless our country and all countries of the world.
Amen.

Halloween

Even though its name—All Hallows Eve—comes from its occurrence on the day before All Saints, the origins of this holiday are pre-Christian. The ancient Celts celebrated the end of the harvest while also ushering in winter, a time of darkness, death, and natural decay. Thus, the costumes and odd traditions, such as the jack-o-lantern, take on a ghoulish flavor.

As children prepare for trick-or-treating and other holiday festivities, send them forth with this prayer of blessing for their safety.

God of Joy,
On Halloween night, keep N._____ and all children safe.
Watch over them and guide them securely home again.
In Jesus' name, I pray.
Amen.

— **ADAPTED FROM *POCKET PRAYERS FOR PARENTS***

Thanksgiving

While it seems obvious that the point of this holiday is to give thanks, the rush and complexity of preparations can often overshadow its original intent. By practicing a ritual dedicated to gratitude, the meaning of the day can be restored. Here are some suggestions:

- Every family member chooses someone for whom they are grateful and then writes a thank-you note to that person.
- Make a centerpiece for the dining table consisting of willow branches, along with pieces of ribbon for each person. During the mealtime blessing, invite everyone to name something or someone for which they are grateful and tie their ribbon on the branches. The centerpiece then becomes a colorful symbol of gratitude.
- Invite each person to use permanent markers to write something on the tablecloth that expresses their gratitude for a blessing in their lives. Bring out the same tablecloth each year as a reminder of the cumulative nature of blessings.

Prayer for Winter Quiet

Spirit of Peace,

There is something soothing about the quiet pace of winter.
The earth's retreat into a time of dormancy
is an invitation to do the same.
In the midst of the daily routines and responsibilities,
guide us towards a place of respite
where we can meet you in silence and solitude.
Let the promise of spring arise in our homes
as we allow the inner soil of our souls to rest and remain still.

May we know your presence throughout this silent season.

Amen.

⇒ ADAPTED FROM *POCKET PRAYERS*
   FOR PARENTS

CHAPTER 4

WHERE
to pray

T he "where" of prayer has long been a critical concern
for religious institutions. Over the centuries, extensive
planning, resources, and creativity have been devoted
to the design of churches and cathedrals, shrines and
synagogues, mosques and monasteries. The most consistent site
for prayer and worship, however, was not a public place, but the
home. The Jewish observance of Shabbat, for example, is a home
ritual that takes place around the table, with blessings recited
over candles, wine, bread, and children. In early Christianity,
families gathered in "house churches" to remember Jesus through
the breaking of bread and reading of the Scriptures.

Many homes today contain some kind of domestic "shrine,"

although its construction may be entirely unintentional. Perhaps it's a Bible, cross, or statue set in a particular place, or the dinner table where grace is offered before meals. In my childhood home, pictures of Jesus and Mary hung in the upstairs hallway. As I passed them while going to and from my bedroom, I felt a sense of comfort in knowing they were somehow present in our family. In the home I built with my husband and children, the coffee table was the focus for several rituals. It was where the seasonal décor was changed to reflect the liturgical cycle, and was thus a natural place for family prayer.

Outside of the home, nature is an ideal setting for contemplation, praise, and thanksgiving. Since so much time is spent in the car, prayers of petition and intercession fit nicely into the movement from one activity to the next. Visits to a church and other sacred places, as well as ones of play and recreation, are also suitable for prayer. In short, we can pray anywhere.

These are all external places for prayer. The greater challenge is creating interior space. This is especially true for parents whose many levels of responsibility at home, at work, and in the community keep them preoccupied and busy. In order for prayer to take hold and flourish, it's vital to establish an interior room in which to nourish the soul and allow it a moment of stillness.

CREATING EXTERNAL SPACE FOR PRAYER

For you, O Lord, have spoken; and with your blessing shall the house of your servant be blessed forever. — 2 SAMUEL 7:29

Our physical environment matters. Not only does it provide the ambience conducive to various practices of prayer, but it also reminds us to be diligent about our spiritual lives. Having a familiar place to go sets rituals in motion without much thought or effort. The *where* becomes the prayer.

Family Prayer Spaces

In the foreword to his classic book *Prayers for the Domestic Church*, Edward Hays notes that every family should select its "shrine-space"—a place to gather together for prayer. This needn't be elaborate, and it should fit within the routine and character of the family. This is why no two domestic shrines look exactly the same.

The most natural place for families to pray is undoubtedly around the table. It is here that we gather to eat meals, play games, do homework or pay bills, and hold discussions. For some families, it may be the only place in which prayer occurs in a formal way. As such, it is a great place for a child's first experience of praying with others. Because it is such a natural space in which to be together—eating, talking, and sharing stories—this learning comes quickly and at an early age.

Making the family table into a shrine-space requires just a few adjustments. Keep it clear of clutter, if possible, and place a few items in the center that can set the tone for a mealtime or seasonal ritual. These can vary over the year, but might include:

- a candle
- a Bible or book of prayers
- a cloth or placemat appropriate to the liturgical or natural season or holiday
- any items for particular rituals, such as a gratitude journal or alms bowl

Personal Prayer Spaces

In addition to a space for communal gathering, every family member needs a place of their own for quiet and reflection. This might be a bedroom, desk, or rocking chair. Even little children enjoy having their own space. Giving them a prayer rug is one way to do this while still keeping them in plain sight. A small patch of carpet, throw rug, or yoga mat can be placed anywhere in the house or yard. It allows a child a bit of time to be still and engaged in prayer of his or her own making. Parents model this when they claim—and use—their own space on a regular basis.

Praying at Church

An obvious place for families to pray together is at church. Just like any ritual, regular attendance on Sunday builds a sense of belonging to a faith community that can't be accomplished by sporadic attendance. To make the coming and going to the Sunday Eucharist more of an intentional ritual, try the following:

Before church:
- Read aloud the gospel and other readings for the liturgy so that children develop a familiarity with them.
- Decide on prayer intentions to offer quietly along with the General Intercessions.
- Encourage young children to watch for a particular gesture of the priest or to listen to and take part in a particular prayer response. Breaking the long liturgy into smaller pieces gives restless children something to focus on.

- Offer a prayer for those who will benefit from the financial offering your family is giving to the parish community.

After church:
- Stay behind and give your child an "up close" look at one of the symbols in the church, such as the baptismal font or tabernacle.
- Take a family poll about something each person is taking away from the liturgy that will inspire them to follow the example of Jesus during the coming week.
- Read over the bulletin and decide on a particular way to contribute to or take part in a parish program that serves those in need.
- Offer a prayer of thanksgiving for your parish.

Prayer Space in the Car

The average American spends over 2½ hours a day in the car. Parents won't be surprised at this figure as so much of their time involves either picking up or dropping off their children at school and other activities.

Saint Christopher was removed from the universal calendar of Catholic saints several years ago but his legend is still pertinent for modern families. The story goes that Christopher, an extremely large man, devoted his life to carrying travelers across a large and

> **Prayer for Driving/Riding in the Car**
>
> *Loving God, keep your hand upon us as we travel, and help us reach our destination in safety.*

formidable stream. One day a child appeared and asked to be carried on Christopher's shoulder. As he made his way across the water, the child grew heavier and heavier. When asked by Christopher for an explanation, the child said he was holding the weight of the world's sins. The child, of course, was Christ. Christopher, whose name means "Christ-carrier," became the patron of travelers.

What an image to keep in mind when shuttling children back and forth! By affirming that Christ lives in our children, the task becomes much more sacred. By focusing on this single task, we might then concentrate more fully on what we are doing.

Enact a small ritual with each car ride. Start with a simple prayer, asking for safe travel, as the seat belts are buckled. When reaching home again, offer another prayer of thanksgiving as the seat belts are unbuckled.

Walking through a Labyrinth

Prayer-walking is a rhythmic and meditative exercise that can take place indoors or out. One of the most calming examples of this is the labyrinth, a circular path made up of "circuits" or routes that lead to a center and then out again. Labyrinths can be found in churches, retreat centers, and parks. It's a wonderful way to foster appreciation for silence as a spiritual practice.

In order to make this a family experience, allow a few minutes between the start of each walker's journey. The three steps involved in praying the labyrinth could be applied to any kind of prayer-walk in which the "center" is the destination point.

• Pausing at the entrance to ask God's blessing

- Pausing at the center to ask for openness to what God has to reveal to us
- Pausing upon exiting to ask God to show us what to take away from the experience

Pilgrimages and Explorations

A pilgrimage is a journey taken to a holy place in order to grow closer to God. Over the centuries, people of all faiths have embarked on such journeys to deepen their spiritual lives and faith. Some take pilgrimages to the Holy Land or to a special church, shrine, temple, or mosque for holy days or times of prayer. The key to making a pilgrimage is being open to the way it changes and strength-

Navajo Prayer

In beauty may I walk;
All day long may I walk;
Through the returning
seasons may I walk.
Beautifully will I possess again
Beautifully birds
Beautifully butterflies...
On the trail marked with pollen
may I walk;
With grasshoppers about my
feet may I walk;
With dew around my feet
may I walk.
With beauty before me
may I walk
With beauty behind me
may I walk
With beauty above me
may I walk
With beauty all around me,
may I walk.
In old age, wandering on a trail
of beauty, lively;
In old age, wandering on a
trail of beauty, living again...
It is finished in beauty.
It is finished in beauty.

ens us by the time we return home. A pilgrimage needn't be to a faraway place, however. There are many ways to take a journey to places we *make* holy by walking in the name of God.

In his book *Care of the Soul*, Thomas Moore places great emphasis on beauty's role in the well-being of the spirit. By exposing children to the beauty of nature, art, music, science, and historical sites, parents cultivate a healthy soulfulness in their children. Along with being pilgrims, families also become explorers—seeking out places in which to walk, ride, play, or pray, remaining ever alert to God's presence.

CREATING INTERNAL SPACE FOR PRAYER

"Whenever you pray, go into your room and shut the door and pray to your Father who is in secret; and your Father who sees in secret will reward you." — MATTHEW 6:6

In Judaism and Christianity, as in other religious traditions, the heart represents treasured beliefs, hopes, loves, and longings. Throughout the Bible, references to the heart depict it as the site of spiritual growth and longing. Scripture mentions the heart more frequently than it does the body, mind, or even the spirit.

Writer and popular speaker Father Richard Rohr points out that, when instructing his disciples about where to pray, Jesus wasn't referring to a physical place. After all, at that time, Jewish families didn't have individual rooms. Instead, he was talking about retreating to an interior space—the "room" of our hearts.

Visiting this heart space on a regular basis is essential to a deep and lasting spirituality. It is a piece of wisdom found in all spiritual traditions. The following four components help to cultivate an interior space, both for families and for individuals:

- Slow down—At some point in the day every family member should take a moment to let activities slow down or stop. Doing so places them in a different kind of time, one not dictated by the clock. By modeling this for children, parents let their actions speak louder than any lectures or dictates. It simply feels good to stop and breathe!

- Be Quiet—Most meditative practices stress the importance of being still. This means eliminating not only external noise but also the internal chatter that sets us on edge. Pay attention to opportunities for small spaces of quiet that fit naturally into a family routine—prior to the mealtime grace or before going to bed, for example.

> **Prayer of Loving Kindness**
>
> *May I be at peace.*
> *May my heart remain open.*
> *May I realize the beauty of my own true nature.*
> *May I be healed.*
> *May I be a source of healing for this world.*
>
> ⇨ TRADITIONAL BUDDHIST PRAYER

- De-clutter—The Reverend Billy Graham once pointed out that he never saw a hearse pulling a U-Haul. It's a vivid reminder about the value as well as the practicality of simplicity. To get to our true needs in prayer, we need to jettison the clutter in our lives. Years ago I learned from a prayerful Franciscan, Sister Jose Hobday, a brilliant formula for a simple life. It involves taking care of ~

    » *all* of our needs

>> *some* of our wants

>> an *occasional* luxury

Try it! You will find it works.

- Pay attention—The Irish phrase "tuning the five-string harp" means opening the senses in order to bring them into alignment with one another. Children are often on sensory overload because of too much noise and visual stimulation. Is it any wonder that so many of them are on medication for an inability to pay attention? The FSSST prayer (Chapter 1) and other centering practices are good ways to practice paying attention. By slowing down, being quiet, and ridding ourselves of extraneous clutter, we pay better attention to the life in and around us. In Buddhist practice, this is called mindfulness. Jesus was saying the same thing when he advised us to turn inward and close the door of the inner heart in order to do *one* thing—be in tune with God.

CHAPTER 5

WHY
pray

t may seem counterintuitive to put the rationale for prayer at the end of this book. Nevertheless, it is only when we know about the practicalities of prayer—the what, how, when, and where—and then start to put those into practice that the value of prayer reveals itself. Once practice becomes familiar and evolves into ritual, the why becomes clear—prayer is good for the soul!

In the midst of all that takes place within a home, prayer calms and grounds us while also widening our perspective. If, as a mother, I know anything about the value of prayer, it is that God will be with me, no matter what. That understanding alone has gotten me through more than one harried day or restless night. It gives me hope.

Prayer as ritual is also vital. It's easy enough to pray on *oh-wow* or even *oh-no* days. Doing so on *ho-hum* days is the tricky part. When ruts and potholes dot the spiritual landscape, ritual keeps us on track. It's an effective way to combat *acedia*, the spiritual laxness that besets even the most ardent pray-er. As a speaker and retreat leader, I often hear from parents and others about the challenges of maintaining a consistent prayer life, particularly within the home. We are busy or distracted by demanding jobs and the responsibilities of domestic life. Kids, as they go through various phases, rebel, and it can be easier to let the whole thing go rather than argue with them. When ritual remains flexible enough to be adapted to such circumstances, it provides a framework for prayer that, in time, becomes part of a family's identity. It's not only what we do, it's who we are.

Someone once described prayer as a way to make friends with God. What a lovely way to describe the intimacy that develops as we enter more deeply into practice. As with any good friend, we turn to God during times of difficulty and doubt, two huge challenges to prayer. In her book *Real Kids, Real Faith*, author Karen Yust notes that the voice of God may come back to us in many different ways, but always within the context of a lifelong friendship. What better rationale for prayer could there be?

MEETING THE CHALLENGE OF PRAYER
Pray in the Spirit at all times in every prayer and supplication.
— EPHESIANS 6:18

Paul's advice to the Ephesians seems simple enough. But what happens when we can't pray? Or when prayer feels dry, lifeless, rote, and uninspired? The truth is that, at some point, each of us will experience periods of distraction, dryness, and dread. By facing such times with prayerful resilience rather than giving up, we eventually find grace in them.

Battling Busyness and Distraction

The busyness of family life is probably the biggest threat to the practice of prayer. Parents are stretched thin with jobs to maintain, households to manage, and children to care for. Add kids' activities, school involvement, and obligations at church and in the community, and there is little time left—for prayer or anything else. Kids are fidgety, adolescents complain, and parents are tempted to chuck the whole thing and opt out.

The benefits of prayer become obvious when we maintain the rituals established around them. The precious five minutes we claim for ourselves in the morning, for example, can make the entire day seem less frantic. The practice of "center-

> **Calming the Distracted Mind**
> When feeling distracted or stressed, the rhythm of a repetitive prayer can soothe and calm the mind and heart. Psalm 136 is an example of this.
>
> *O give thanks to the Lord, for he is good,*
> *for his steadfast love*
> *endures forever.*
>
> *O give thanks to the God of gods,*
> *for his steadfast love*
> *endures forever.*
>
> *O give thanks to the Lord of lords,*
> *for his steadfast love*
> *endures forever...*

ing"—through being mindful of the breath or using a repetitive psalm, for example—helps children and adolescents cope when feeling fearful, anxious, or stressed. More than anything, prayer as a continual practice reminds us that we can call upon God for help, guidance, comfort, or strength wherever we are and whatever we are doing. Rather than expecting our prayers to sound a particular way, God is always ready, like a best friend, to listen.

Dealing with a child or adolescent who is restless, bored, or resistant during times of family prayer can also be a challenge, as well as a distraction, to the rest of the family. Here are some suggestions for dealing with such situations:

- Involve your child in planning the ritual, perhaps by decorating the space, writing a prayer, or finding a piece of music.
- Talk to your child after a restless episode to find out what he or she is finding difficult or boring. Resist the temptation to correct or mandate attention. Ask for ideas about how to make the ritual more relevant and/or interesting.
- Rituals that aren't adaptive are deadly. Pay attention to your child's developmental needs and interests, as well as his or her personality. Some children are natural contemplatives; others find it much more engaging to be doing something. By adapting rituals according to the age and interest level of your child, prayer becomes more relevant, interesting, and engaging.

Countering Acedia

Saint Catherine of Siena described acedia as less a matter of "spiritual laziness" and more of spiritual depression. It occurs, she said, as a result of exhaustion, worry, and feeling overwhelmed.

These are realities parents and families know all too well.

As with mild mental depression, there are ways to deal with acedia that manage and eventually extract us from it. We know, for example, that physical exercise, laughter, and certain foods release endorphins. These feel-good hormones, when released into the brain, relieve depression. In similar fashion, there are "spiritual endorphins" that

> *You, O Eternal Trinity,*
> *are a deep sea into which,*
> *the more I enter,*
> *the more I find.*
> *And the more I find,*
> *the more I seek.*
>
> — **SAINT CATHERINE OF SIENA**

counteract the effects of acedia. A gratitude journal (Chapter 1) or exploration of beauty (Chapter 4) are two of them. Another is to ignore how you feel and "just do it"—that is, to engage in a prayer practice, attend church, or meditate for five minutes. Any discipline, be it athletic or aesthetic, runs into walls of resistance. The best thing is to climb over them and move forward.

Dealing with Change

A great benefit of rituals is how they help us through life passages. Think of a beautiful wedding ceremony and how it facilitates letting go of a child and celebrating the changes in a family. At the other end of the spectrum is the comfort derived from a funeral in which, through prayer and storytelling, we grieve the loss of a loved one.

Offering together traditional or spontaneous prayers can move a family through transitions with greater hope and ease.

By turning to God for guidance and support, change becomes an opportunity for growth and grace.

Encountering Grief, Loss, and Disappointment

We cannot protect ourselves or our children from loss. It is part of the human experience, be it the death of a loved one, the erosion of health, or the devastation of divorce. The way to deal with it, and eventually find healing, is through grieving. Over the centuries, humans have devised a number of rituals to move through and past the stages of mourning. Over time, they restore a sense of peace, even if the hole in our lives is never completely filled in again.

At such times prayer can either flow freely out of the depth of our pain or remain stilted and stifled due to anger or depression. Praying our way through grief, loss, or disappointment sharpens our recognition of God's presence in even the most distressing aspects of life.

Prayer during a Time of Change

Creator God,
Change is disrupting our
  family's routines.
During this time, remind
  us that chaos often
  precedes creation.
Grant us your peace and
  hope for the future.
Move us through this
  change with grace so
  that, in time,
we find new life in our
  family.
With belief in creative
  possibility, we pray.
Amen.

— ADAPTED FROM *POCKET PRAYERS FOR PARENTS*

The people of the Bible understood that all prayers can and should be brought to God—even those of anger, grief, and disappointment. Thus, more than a third of the Book of Psalms are laments. In addition, an entire book in the Old Testament—the Book of Lamentations—is devoted to these sorrowful prayers. At times they are full of complaints and self-pity. Other times they are full of devastation and despair, as those offering them deal with death, exile, and the fear of abandonment. God hears them all.

Biblical prayers of lament are comprised of five components. Each one can be adapted within the family as a way to express the grief, disappointment, heartache, or hopelessness that we experience personally or that we see happening in the world around us.

1. Invoking God's presence. To invoke means to "call upon" and is a form of supplication. We address God in a way that represents our understanding of God in the midst of our distress. While any form of prayer can include an invocation, prayers of lament use those that express desperation or longing, such as *"My God, my God, why have you forsaken me?"* (Psalm 22:1), the psalm that Jesus prayed while dying on the cross.

> *"Learning to lament could be one means by which children discover that, with God, they are no longer alone or powerless."*
> — KAREN YUST

2. Naming the grief, loss, or disappointment we are suffering. Imagine what it would be like to have your city, your home, and everything you cherish destroyed. This is the agonizing situation of the Hebrew people during the destruction of Jerusalem and its temple in the 6th century BC. *"Look and see our disgrace!...We have become orphans, fatherless; our mothers are like widows"* (Lamentations 5:1, 3). The familial images in this cry of mourning are especially touching. They speak of loss, abandonment, and the surrender of all hope. Many of us were taught "polite" prayers that were devoid of any complaints or expressions of anger or disappointment. Prayers of lament aren't polite; they're *real*. Encouraging children and adolescents to bring all of their hurts, fears, disillusionment, anger, and concerns to God fosters deeper intimacy and uncovers the meaning of true faith.

3. Expressing confidence or trust in God's responsive love. I am fond of calling the Psalms a book of mixed emotions. Take Psalm 139. It's my favorite psalm, one that extols God for his wonderful works, including the intricacies of the human person. Without warning, it takes off on a rant about *"hating those who hate you..."* (verse 21). Then it turns round again with the plea, *"Search me, O God, and know my heart; test me and know my thoughts"* (verse 23). Troubled prayers often end up a jumble of emotions. While they may run the gamut from despair to delight, God's constancy remains intact. This does not mean we will reach this stage of lament in a single prayer. It comes with time and attentiveness as we hold onto hope in God's unconditional love.

4. Requesting explicit help for our troubles. Biblical writers didn't beat around the bush. They knew what they needed and asked God for it in no uncertain terms, even if it sounds horribly cruel and vengeful. Psalm 139 asks God to *"kill the wicked,"* and the writer of Lamentations asks for *"anguish of heart"* (3:65) as payback for those who wrought such destruction on Jerusalem. As parents, we're understandably wary of encouraging our children to pray in such violent terms. Nevertheless, there is a human need to give voice to our hurts and frustration without smothering them in platitudes. The help we request might be the cultivation of compassion, understanding, tolerance, or hope. Doing so expands our capacity for empathy. It also offers a way to cope with injustice without denying it, nor of excusing abusive behavior on the part of others.

5. Praising God for bringing us through our lament. One of the most mysterious aspects of the Christian faith is our belief in resurrection—of life coming out of death, light emanating from darkness. Anyone who has found "grace in the wound" knows that we stand to learn much from the suffering in our lives. This last component of lamentation has to come in its own time and cannot be rushed or forced. This is especially important to remember when we are tempted to press a child beyond a hurtful situation before he or she is ready. Karen Yust notes that helping children move through the stages of lament provides a way to both name their feelings about what is wrong with the world, as well as to imagine how things could be better.

FINDING PEACE IN PRAYER

Peace I leave with you,
my peace I give to you.

⇒ JOHN 14:27

Finding peace may be one of the biggest of all rationales for prayer. Who doesn't long for serenity instead of stress, for calm in the midst of crisis? Within the ups and downs of family life, prayer and ritual provide safe harbor. One of the most well-known prayers for peace and consolation is Psalm 23. Is it any wonder that it is chosen frequently for funerals? By combining this lovely prayer with the intake and exhalation of breath, it becomes a meditative experience that soothes mind and body.

So, too, is the Our Father. Breathing in with one line and breathing out with the next makes this familiar prayer a calming reflection on God's holy name, power and pres-

Prayer of Peace

"Peace I leave with you;
my peace I give to you."
(John 14:27)

Holy Spirit of Peace,
settle deep within
*   our hearts.*
Enliven our actions
*   with gentleness and*
*   thoughtfulness.*
Let the words we
*   speak resonate*
*   with compassion*
*   and caring.*
Help us to bear one
*   another's burdens,*
*   if only in part,*
so that we become
*   sacred instruments*
*   of your peace.*
May we inhale your
*   wisdom and exhale*
*   your grace.*
In Jesus' blessed name,
*   we pray.*
Amen.

ence, generosity and mercy, and everlasting goodness. Here is how to craft a family meditation with this beloved prayer.

- If using the prayer with other family members, take a moment to quiet yourselves.
- Eliminate distractions and invite everyone to find a comfortable place to sit.
- One person might recite the prayer slowly or everyone might say it together.
- With each line or phrase breathe in and out as follows:

[Breathe in slowly] *Our Father, who art in heaven,*

[Breathe out slowly] *hallowed be thy name.*

[Breathe in slowly] *Thy kingdom come;*

[Breathe out slowly] *thy will be done*

[Breathe in slowly] *on earth*

[Breathe out slowly] *as it is in heaven.*

[Breathe in slowly] *Give us this day*

[Breathe out slowly] *our daily bread.*

[Breathe in slowly] *Forgive us our trespasses*

[Breathe out slowly] *as we forgive those who trespass against us.*

[Breathe in slowly] *Lead us not into temptation,*

[Breathe out slowly] *but deliver us from evil.*

[Breathe in and out slowly] *Amen.*

CREATING HARMONY IN THE MIDST OF CHAOS

When families experience overload, any little incident can trigger a round of bickering that frazzles the nerves and cuts a parent's capability for patience in half. Multiple activities generate havoc that, in turn, adds to a continual thrum of tension. This only ramps up the potential for arguments. Eventually, the whole family can be drawn into the maelstrom.

Dolores Curran describes the value of rituals in her book *Tired of Arguing with Your Kids*, by noting the calming

> *"When rituals become second nature to children, order and harmony reign, but when rituals are absent, the result is disorder and havoc, fertile breeding ground for family conflict.*
> — **DOLORES CURRAN**

effect they create in the midst of chaos. While setting rules alleviates some of the arguments that crop up in family life, rituals hold additional impact through their reliability and solidity. Most family rituals arise out of daily routines and take hold over time. They are rarely discussed or planned out, but simply become part of a day's interaction. As Curran notes, rituals reduce the need for arguments because something unstated has moved into place. It might be as mundane as clearing the dinner table or as highly crafted as the celebration of a holiday, such as Thanksgiving. Either way, rituals provide a safe haven in the midst of havoc.

When parents become mindful of the rituals that have become part of domestic life, they can also seize upon them as opportunities for prayer and reflection. Daily rituals provide a sense of flow that keeps turning our hearts and minds to God's grace and love. Seasonal rituals and those associated with events and milestones provide opportunities to celebrate the love and relationships that hold families together.

Spirit of Kindness,
Sometimes it's hard to remain calm in the midst
of family chaos.
People come and go and leave behind a trail of debris.
It leaves all of us tired and frustrated.
When tempted to close ourselves off or explode in anger,
give us pause.
Remind us to breathe deeply.
And help us to remember that chaos is the prelude to creation.
With faith in your power and grace, we pray.
Amen.
➤ **ADAPTED FROM** *POCKET PRAYERS FOR PARENTS*

Closing thoughts

One of my friends once told me about the effort she put into learning a particular form of prayer. It required a lot of time, focus, and an ability to be still—all of which were in short supply in her house full of children. After several frustrated attempts at making it a regular practice, she began to berate herself over what she perceived was a failure. She sought out a monk who gave her some sage advice: *"Don't pray what you can't; pray what you can."*

I am well aware that the material in this book is only a smattering of what family prayer can entail. Some of it will fit your family while other parts may feel awkward and contrived. In the case of the latter, I encourage you to follow the monk's counsel by praying what you can. In any case, to be genuine, family prayer and ritual must be your own.

I also encourage parents to see ourselves as planters of seeds. Guiding children in prayer takes a relinquishment of expectation. Even when they rebel, resist, and retreat down paths far from our choosing, we can place hope that the seeds are still there, awaiting the right season to take root. In the end, we must let them go and trust that they are being watched over by a God who loves and knows them far better than we do.

In the meantime, the cultivation of prayer must be something we undertake for ourselves. As a parent, I honestly don't know how I would make it without the strength, assurance, and peace that prayer brings me. It gives me insight when everything looks murky, and keeps me steady when the ground beneath me shifts. It leads me to forgive when I feel betrayed and to move on when I am tempted to wallow in self-pity. Rituals have given me a way to celebrate the large and small moments of my life and that of my nuclear and extended family. They also kept us intact during our rough days, and provided continuity during periods of tumult and change.

Prayer has lifted my heart and brought me to tears. It has driven me to my knees, and compelled me to dance. It is the best way I know to meet the challenge and cherish the joy of being a family.

Favorite family prayers and rituals

_____

_____

_____

_____

_____

_____

_____

_____

_____

_____

Other prayer resources

Pocket Prayers for Parents
KATHY HENDRICKS

A treasury of prayers for the many wondrous and often baffling experiences of parenthood that inspire, comfort, and support today's busy parents as they celebrate occasions and milestones, face transitions or crises, or to simply catch their breath.

80 PAGES | $9.95 | 978-1-58595-936-5

Keeping the Faith
Prayers for College Students
KERRY WEBER

Kerry Weber beautifully expresses all the familiar emotions that every college student experiences. A wonderful gift for any young person heading off to college

64 PAGES | $5.95 | 978-1-58595-738-5

Pocket Prayers for Young Professionals
JULIE RATTEY

More than 100 prayers for the many emotions and situations young professionals encounter include coping with stress, starting a new job, dealing with work issues, celebrating success, and much more. Filled with warmth, wit, and wisdom—a wonderfully illuminating book!

80 PAGES | $9.95 | 978-1-58595-939-6

A Prayerbook for Eucharistic Adoration
DANIEL CONNORS

The prayers and reflections in this powerful book capture the awe, joy, and wonder of every moment in the presence of the Living God. A meaningful companion for anyone who wishes to spend time in the Real Presence of Christ.

64 PAGES | $9.95 | 978-1-58595-923-5
QUALITY FRENCH FLAP BINDING

1-800-321-0411
www.23rdpublications.com

TWENTY THIRD 23rd
PUBLICATIONS